Chinese Music and Orchestration:
A Primer on Principles and Practice

Chinese Music Monograph Series
ISSN: 1071-5649

Series Editors:
Yuan-Yuan Lee Ph.D.
Sin-yan Shen Ph.D.

- **CHINESE MUSIC AND ORCHESTRATION:**
  A Primer on Principles and Practice

- **CHINESE MUSICAL INSTRUMENTS**

- **CHINA:** *A Journey into Its Musical Art*

- **WHAT MAKES CHINESE MUSIC CHINESE?**
  Theory, Compositions and Analysis

- **MUSICIANS OF CHINESE MUSIC**

- **THE REGIONAL MUSIC OF CHINA**

- **CHINESE MUSIC IN THE 20TH CENTURY**

- **RITUAL MUSIC IN A NORTH CHINA VILLAGE:**
  The Continuing Confucian and Buddhist Heritage

Chinese Music and Orchestration:
A Primer on Principles and Practice

SIN-YAN SHEN

Chinese Music Society of North America
Chicago   USA

CHINESE MUSIC AND ORCHESTRATION: A PRIMER ON PRINCIPLES
AND PRACTICE
Copyright Chinese Music Society of North America, Chicago, USA, 1991
First Edition, 1991
Third Printing, 2005

Published in the United States of America by the Chinese Music Society of North
America, P.O. Box 5275, Woodridge IL 60517-0275 USA.

All rights reserved. No part of this book may be reproduced or utilized in any form or by
any means, electronic or mechanical, including photocopying, recording, or by any
information storage or retrieval systems, without the written permission from the
publisher.

Library of Congress Catalog Card Number 91-75864

Library of Congress Cataloging in Publication Data
Shen, Sin-yan, 1949-
Chinese Music and Orchestration: A Primer on Principles and Practice
ISBN 1-880464-00-4
1. Music.   2. China.   3. Orchestration.   4. Compositions.
5. Acoustics   6. Instruments   I. Title   II. Series

Chinese Music Monograph Series books and Chinese Music Masterpiece CD Series are
available at special discounts when purchased in bulk quantity for institutions, business,
and associations. Recordings of musical works cited are also available. Contact the
Chinese Music Society of North America, P.O. Box 5275, Woodridge IL 60517-0275
USA.

CONTENTS

AUTHOR'S NOTE   v

WHAT MAKES CHINESE MUSIC CHINESE?
           1

A MOST COMPREHENSIVE SET OF HARMONIES, 2
THE CHINESE QUALITY OF MUSIC, 10
CONCLUSION, 13

FOUNDATIONS OF THE CHINESE ORCHESTRA
           14

INTRODUCTION, 14
BASIS SET AND TONALITY, 16
TYPES OF ORCHESTRAS, 21
THE USE OF THE STRINGS, 31
THE SANXIAN'S, 32
YANGQIN, 35
SHENG, 37
THE DOUBLE REEDS, 41
REFERENCES, 43

ON THE ACOUSTICAL SPACE OF THE CHINESE ORCHESTRA
           45

INTRODUCTION, 45
THE ORCHESTRA'S TONAL SPECTRUM AND ITS

ARTISTIC UTILIZATION, 46
   First Fundamental Spectrum - the Shengguan, 48
   Second Fundamental Spectrum - the Tanbo, 50
   Considerations for the Special Colors, 54
THE LANGUAGE OF THE MUSIC, 56
CONCLUSION, 58
BIBLIOGRAPHY, 60

THE ACOUSTICS OF WIND INSTRUMENTS - A Study in Resonator Design and Performance of Guanyue

61

INTRODUCTION, 62
COUPLED SYSTEMS OF AIR COLUMN AND REEDED EXCITATION, 63
A MAJOR SCIENTIFIC DISCOVERY: THE TRANSVERSE FLUTE, 65
THE SOUND OF THE SINGLE FREE REED, 67
HARMONY AND MELODY, 69
MUSIC OF THE DOUBLE REED, 71
THE ENSEMBLE AND ORCHESTRAL ROLES, 72
REFERENCES, 76

ORCHESTRATION WITH CHINESE PERCUSSION INSTRUMENTS

80

OVERVIEW, 80
FUNCTIONS AND PERFORMANCE TECHNIQUES, 81
ORCHESTRATION TECHNIQUES, 89
BIBLIOGRAPHY, 99

THE TANTIAO (PIPA) STRINGS

100

THE NEW PLUCKED STRINGS - TANTIAO SYSTEM, 102
THE INFLUENCE OF THE RUAN ON THE PIPA, 109
HULEI - A HYBRID TANTIAO STRING, 112
CONCLUSION, 113
REFERENCES, 114

ON THE SYSTEM OF CHINESE FIDDLES
117

GENERAL DISCUSSION, 117
ERHU - THE MOST POPULAR SECOND FIDDLE, 118
THE ARTISTRY OF THE CHINESE FIDDLES, 120
ENSEMBLE ROLES OF THE CHINESE FIDDLES, 125
SPECIAL NOTES ON THE CHINESE FIDDLE CLASSIFICATION, 127
REFERENCES, 130

THE SHANGHAI TRADITIONAL ORCHESTRA AND HE WU-QI
132

INTRODUCTION, 132
HE WU-QI - A DYNAMIC DIRECTOR, 133
FUTURE IN PERSPECTIVE, 139
REFERENCES, 144

APPENDIX I: INSTRUMENTS OF THE ORCHESTRA
145

INDEX
155

AUTHOR'S NOTE

Material for this book has been developed over the years teaching at the graduate and the undergraduate levels and at the Research Institute of the Chinese Music Society of North America.

Pursuing our exploration of the almost limitless caverns of Chinese music and orchestration, so much of which has never yet come to the knowledge of the rest of the world, we approach the subject from both the angles of principles and practice. Functional discussions of musical interest, cultural molding of musical psychology, instrumental effects and acoustics are emphasized. The exploration centers on the principle of cultural acoustics, that is the impacts of musical acoustics is strongly modified by our ear and brain which are products of culture.

The intended audience are students of music at the university level, and music practitioners. The book is written so that it requires no prior knowledge of Chinese music or acoustics. Also, no knowledge of the Chinese language is assumed.

With the opening chapter we find ourselves at a focal point in the present study: What Makes Chinese Music Chinese? The cultural preference of harmony, and thus intervals and tones and rhythms used in music, distinguishes one music from another. Chinese music, however, is unique in its uninterrupted history of more than 8000 years and very early development of theoretical systematics, acoustical and material science, and orchestral practice.

The Chinese orchestra is not a single species, but rather several dozens of acoustically unified and musically interesting orchestras, primarily based on reeded wind and plucked strings as orchestral tone quality bases. The foundations of the Chinese orchestra is the subject of the second and the third chapters. The four principal instrumental subgroups of reeded wind, percussion, plucked string, and bowed string are then studied in detail in four chapters. The orchestral roles, acoustics, performance practice, orchestration techniques and repertoire of each group form the key areas of discussion. Numerous practical examples are used throughout to aid the discussion.

The practice of the Shanghai Traditional Orchestra, one of the very best in the world, is the subject of the final chapter, dealing with orchestral practice.

A detailed discussion of the instruments of the Chinese orchestra in the Appendix complements the text.

In the first two chapters where a philosophical overview is presented and where most of the principal instruments are first introduced, the Chinese names of the instruments are italicized.

It is a pleasure to offer public gratitude to those who have shaped this work. Throughout this research and writing, Dr. Yuan-Yuan Lee provided detailed and thought-provoking critique of the discussion concerning every concept and every analysis. Many years ago Dr. Shan S. Wong suggested that I write this book. Colleagues in theory, composition, and performance throughout the world had stimulated the completion of this text. The masters of Chinese music and acoustical masters throughout the ages inspired my theoretical and practical approach.

I specially thank my parents for without their constant encouragements and guidance over the years this work would not have been possible, and without the open-minded cultural environment provided by them in my youth the subject of cultural acoustics would not have appeared.

> I   do
> II   re
> III mi
> IV   fa
> V   sol
> VI   la
> VII ti
> VIII do

What Makes Chinese Music Chinese?

WHAT MAKES CHINESE MUSIC CHINESE?[1]

The music of the Chinese people is analyzed from the perspectives of harmony, musical structure, and music appreciation. New results are presented on an extensive harmonic analysis of the Chinese musical system. The musical subsystems of China are unified through a comprehensive system of five basic harmonies. The question of "what makes Chinese music Chinese?" is addressed from both a theoretical and a performance point of view. The criticality of tonal requirement is examined using orchestrational and individual virtuosic-interpretive examples. The important achievements of the Chinese musical system and its versatility are discussed.

To address the question of "what makes Chinese music Chinese?" I propose to systematically introduce the fundamental building blocks of the Chinese musical system. As we go along, I shall attempt to stimulate your perception of the very creative and cultural aspects of the music. After all, music is intrinsically a cultural fulfillment, and a field of unlimited human creativity.

---

[1] Originally published in *Chinese Music*, Vol. 4, No. 2 (1981).

Chinese Music and Orchestration

Speaking of culture, the Chinese culture, or for that matter any cultural system, represents a set of ways of doing things, a set of preferences. Historically as the set of ways of doing things evolves, the power of human creativity takes precedence, and the best part of life is brought out in front of us - a great piece of music stimulates your mind, and has the ability to help you concentrate on the important things in life, and to help you overcome obstacles in life.

China is a vast country. Over the ages, a great many scale systems have evolved in different geographical regions. But one thing unifies these musical subsystems into a Chinese musical system - the Chinese preference of harmony.

A MOST COMPREHENSIVE SET OF HARMONIES

Let us examine the Chinese set of ways of doing things - their order of preference of musical intervals and chords. Acoustics is cultural. Here I will elaborate on my nomenclature as I go along.

Do you know the earliest musical interval documented in human history? This very same interval which is 7000 years old now still exists today. This interval is contained on a *xun*, globular flute, unearthed in this century. It is a minor third!

This interval is still well loved by the Chinese people today. Take an example from Qinqiang, theatrical music of Shaanxi:

What Makes Chinese Music Chinese?

The preference of minor third and major sixth masks the semitones, and as a result the scale becomes unclear to the Western ear. Some people have mistakenly thought that scale was pentatonic. It really is heptatonic:

During the many thousands of years a complete system of harmonic structures has evolved. These harmonic structures are the most basic building blocks of Chinese music. They are what I call the *basis set*, from which the whole musical harmonic space can be generated.

A frequently encountered harmonic structure, which has a long, long history is the zhi harmony:

lower tonic - subdominant - dominant (so - do - re - so)

Within a given octave, the zhi harmony utilizes the tonic (so or sol), the subdominant (do), and the dominant (re) as the most stable skeleton structure to produce the tonic chord known as zhi. The basis set members and other members of the scale (tone sequence) are shown below:

or

Chinese Music and Orchestration

or

I will illustrate the use of this structure by doing a section of a song: "Zhou Jiangzhou".

In this example the basis set structure dominates the melodic progression. It is an extreme case of the zhi harmony, but serves as a clear illustration of the use of the harmonic members in designing the melodic skeleton. In "Zhou Jiangzhou", an ancient heptatonic scale is used:

What Makes Chinese Music Chinese?

Of closest relation to the zhi harmony is the shang harmony:

re - so - la - re
II V   VI II

The scale for the octave would look like:

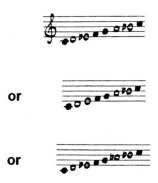

"Cuihu Chunxiao" (Spring at the Emerald Lake) is written with a dominance of the shang harmony:

This is an example of a side cadence. In traditional Chinese musical terminology, there is a difference between "zheng sha" (cadence) and "ce

Chinese Music and Orchestration

"ce sha"

sha" (side cadence). In side cadence, the ending does not occur at the tonic, but rather borrows another member of the basis set to stop.

The next harmony is the yu harmony:

    la - re - mi - la
    VI II III VI

Filling in other notes of the scale it ascends like:

or

or

These three harmony structures are established on the basis of the fourths and the fifths. Within the octave, the fifth is incorporated and within the fifth, a fourth is added.

I said in the beginning that the minor third was the first interval. So where is it?

It plays rather important roles in the jue and the gong harmony. The jue harmony is:

    mi - la - do - mi
    III VI I III

What Makes Chinese Music Chinese?

With other members of the scale, the full octave is:

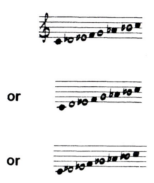

The dominant in the jue harmony is a minor six, and a fourth is placed within this minor six. If you examine closely, this is probably a very familiar harmony to you. It is an inversion of the minor triad. The jue harmony is quite different from the tonic-subdominant-dominant structure or the tertian structure. Had it been constructed using a tonic-subdominant-dominant structure, it would look like:

    mi - la - ti - mi
    III VI VII III

and if it had a tertian structure, it would be:

    mi - so - ti - mi
    III V VII III

The gong harmony is:

    do - mi - so - do
    I III V I

Chinese Music and Orchestration

with a scale of:

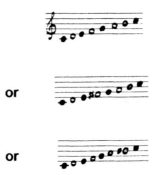

Superficially, this last harmony of the five basis sets looks exactly the same as the major triad. But functionally, the second inversion of gong is more emphasized than its Western counterpart.

Let us examine all five harmonies together. What do we observe?

(harmonies:)

    (zhi: so-do-re-so)

        (shang: re-so-la-re)

            (yu: la-re-mi-la)

                (jue: mi-la-do-mé)

                    (gong: do-mi-so-do)

What Makes Chinese Music Chinese?

The sequence form a cyclic system which generates itself. These are the underlying building blocks of the Chinese musical system. A highly creative and flexible system of techniques, for variations of color and tonality, is imbedded in this cyclic system. Further this system has been practiced by countless musicians over the ages, and that represents a tremendous accumulation of human experience in one field.

It must be emphasized, the set of ways of doing things, the rules governing how things get done, only begins to manifest itself after a long period of human practice. The creativity guides practices. Then comes theory, after which there is room for further creativity, room for you to explore the intrinsic magic of the system. This is how real music evolves.

Once again, these five harmonies have often been confused by researchers with a so-called "pentatonic scale". Pentatonic scale is a term without any real practical meaning here. Chinese music does not conform to any pentatonic scale. It is the harmonic preference (the cultural acoustics) described above that makes Chinese music Chinese, and unifies all scale systems loved and practiced by the Chinese people.

The Chinese musical system has a unified system of a most comprehensive set of five harmonic structures: zhi, shang, yu, jue, gong. For comparison purposes, the Western classical music system also has a unified system of two harmonic structures: major and minor:

do - mi - so - do

la - do - mi - la

In both, a fifth is always present in each octave, and depending on whether a major third or a minor third is inserted in the fifth, the harmony is major, or minor.

Chinese Music and Orchestration

Both, an octave and a fifth, are physically harmonious intervals. But good music depends on one's ability to strike a balance between harmony and discord. So other intervals can become important. In Chinese music, factors of fourths and thirds both play important functional roles, whereas in Western music, the emphasis is placed on a tertian (of degree three) system. There is intrinsically more freedom built into the Chinese musical system. To extend this discussion further, a fourth has a fifth as its complement with respect to the octave, and has a major second as its complement with respect to the fifth. A major third has a minor sixth as its complement with respect to the octave, and a minor third as its complement with respect to the fifth.

THE CHINESE QUALITY OF MUSIC

The Chinese people have, since remote days, considered musical expression a very high form of human interaction. A best friend, for instance, in Chinese is known as "zhi yin". "Zhi" here stands for to know or to appreciate. "Yin" is sound, or message. So if we are good friends, you got the message! "Yin" and "yue" together make up music. We just explained "yin". "Yue" is happiness or joy. In what form is musical joy expressed? What are the qualities of music that the Chinese people treasure? What is their preference of musical expression?

Compared with ways of musical expression in the European and the American tradition, Chinese music is more implicit, but at the same time less restrained, in expression: that mental activity conveyed through the expansion of the music, the tonal contrast, and the tonal manipulation carry very far, and is beyond description, by words or by visual art.

What Makes Chinese Music Chinese?

The Chinese people cares more about feeling, and respect appreciation more than anything else. It is a usual practice that a lot of the music have titles, but the music is intrinsically non-programmatic.

This brings up the point of "yi". To the Chinese musician, a good piece of music expresses not the scenery, but the yi - the artistic conception. And to this end, tonal manipulation represents the ability to musically speak.

Take for example, "Music at Sunset" as performed by the Shanghai Traditional Orchestra - the best recording of the piece by the way. It begins with

The exact same note on the score is generated three completely different ways on the pipa to stimulate tonal interest. Then pauses:

This is followed by

Chinese Music and Orchestration

⌐o o⌐ : *indefinite number of repetitions*

The highly embellished

on the *zheng* (the horizontal open-string zither) creates the most fascinating effect you can imagine.

Recently, I heard the Boston Symphony performing a tone poem version of "Music at Sunset" under Seiji Ozawa. It would have been alright if you considered that version a brand new piece, having nothing what-so-ever to do with "Music at Sunset". But its melodic materials were completely extracted from "Music at Sunset", and after knowing too well that the recording of the Shanghai Traditional Orchestra exists, the Boston Symphony version sounds so utterly bland and tasteless! I guess the one really to blame is the arranger for the Boston version. He treated the music as if there is only plain melody, and no orchestrational input, no tonal fascination, what-so-ever.

Tone is also the most important element in solo music. The *qin* (fingerboard zither) has two to three hundred notations for tonal requirement, and *qin* musicians are continuously generating more as needs arise. Tone is the most desired quality in musical interpretation for a large category of Chinese music. It is part of the melodic flow.

What Makes Chinese Music Chinese?

The Chinese musicians are a most sensitive breed. They are perceptive of the most minute variation in tonal inflection, the change in the degree of embellishment of a motive, and the slightest tonal and dynamic contrast that occur in a composition. Traditionally, Chinese compositions have been largely written in multi-part form. A musical idea has to be developed to full bloom before the musical joy is conveyed. Philosophically, the composers treasured the feelings of joy and friendship which occurred in certain periods of their life, and viewed such feeling as eternal joy and encouragements. The "yue" in "yin yue" (music) conveys this joy, and its implication in the area of entertainment is very low. In contrast, Western classical music in all categories, was written with more entertainment purposes in mind. It was a result of a work-for-hire system.

CONCLUSION

We analyzed the music of the Chinese people from the perspectives of harmony, structure, and music appreciation. All theory, and descriptions of results, are presented as a systematic summary of an accumulation of experience. It is there for the purpose of information transfer. It is there so that newcomers in the field could gain an easier start and make better contributions. No theory should become a constraint on creativity.

In today's age of rapid information transfer, every citizen of the world, with sufficient effort, should have the right to enjoy the fruits of human civilization, whether it was created in China, in Europe, or elsewhere, and all of us have the obligation to make accessible not only the fruit, but also the flow of thought, and the cause and consequences, which led to the fruit.

Chinese Music and Orchestration

FOUNDATIONS OF THE CHINESE ORCHESTRA[2]

We attempt to examine the important elements of musical forms, harmony, and orchestration practices which constitute the functional and structural makeup of the Chinese orchestra.

INTRODUCTION

China is a multi-national state with a highly diversified culture. As researchers of Chinese music well know, the greatest difficulty one encounters in studying the music of the Chinese people is in fact in understanding and getting the right feeling for the large number of different harmony systems which have coexisted with one another and influenced one another, with a history of many thousands of years.

Here we must first of all define what we mean by a harmony system. The term harmony system is used to encompass the scale structure, the arpeggio structure, structure of the melodic progression and contrapuntal practices, which together define the cultural preference of a music system, such as the Chinese system, the European system or the

---

[2] Originally published in two parts in *Chinese Music*, Vol. 2, No. 3 (1979) and Vol. 3, No. 1 (1980).

Foundations of the Chinese Orchestra

American system. In addition to the harmony system, there are factors which govern the cultural implication of a musical system. They include musical forms, rhythmic practices and tempo structure. In essence, the harmony system of a music system consists of those properties which make up the concept of harmoniousness. The concept of harmoniousness differs from culture to culture; the octaves, fifths and fourths are harmonious by physical nature, but the order in which a musical culture prefers intervals other than the above ones is highly cultural-dependent.

Ultimately, music is a culture-independent human creation. True music lovers, who by default always have more experience in one cultural system than others, will appreciate the artistic value and the virtuosity of a top notch musical performance, no matter what the cultural background of the performer may be. This phenomenon however represents a very high level of human communication, and does not take place on an everyday basis.

The most important property which pertains to a harmony system is probably that of *diaoxing* (tonality). The *diaoxing* of a musical passage is the actual musical color which a listener familiar with the passage perceives. The musical color conveyed by a music is certainly a subjective property under a single experiment, but the accumulated result of a large number of experiments is often non-zero, especially if the experiments were carried out with listeners of similar cultural background. Individuals brought up under the environment of Peking opera, for instance, can immediately tell if a musical passage indeed sounds like Peking opera, because he recognizes the special color which Peking opera conveys. Further, the preference of musical tonality of a culture, to a fairly large extent, implicitly defines the concept of harmoniousness of the culture.

Chinese Music and Orchestration

BASIS SET AND TONALITY

What in musical terms defines the tonality of a music? We will discuss this question through the examination of a number of examples. "Dui Hua" (Flower Riddles) is a very popular piece in Northern China. Any piece that is as popular as "Dui Hua" usually have a number of versions, but the key passages which characterize the spirit of the music are obviously present in all versions. These include:

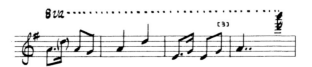

its answering phrase:

and the other important half which includes the percussion pattern:

Foundations of the Chinese Orchestra

The melodic progression of "Dui Hua" presents a most dominant note, A. The secondarily dominant notes are D and E. This is more clearly seen if we remove the decorative notes and examine:

Here G is an unstable tone, and tends to move towards A as seen in the measures [3] and [4]. Similarly the B in measure [7] is mobile and leads to A. The role played by the set of notes ADEA is rather crucial, as they define the cadences of the music. Their importance in the structural makeup of the music is equal to that of $AC^\#EA$ in the Western A major scale. The notes in the basis set of a passage not only appear to be more stable and dominant while we appreciate the tonality of the music, but also occur as the most popular melodic sequence other than the primary scale of the music. The basis set used in a music makes up more than fifty percent of the tonality appearance of music, the remaining ingredients being the "hua," or decorative ornaments which musically links one note to another to form a melodic progression. Take measures [7] and [8] in the answering phrase of "Dui Hua" for example, the skeleton is:

and with the decoration of C and G, the full progression in measures [7] and [8] is formed and conveys a Huabei (Northern China) color.

Chinese Music and Orchestration

We must emphasize that our analysis here is merely necessary in the initial approach to a music which may be totally unfamiliar to the person analyzing it. The results are not to be taken as mechanical formulas. In this respect of an attempt to understand Chinese music, feeling based on long time exposure is most important, as music is an art and not an emotionless science.

The structure of the melodic progressions in China are very different from one region to another. We will analyze this aspect of the Chinese harmony system in relation to the basis set of notes for the different modes as a later stage.

Another feature must be included on the examination list when one analyses Chinese music; that is the ornamentation of the performer. The large number of grace notes, d^1 in measure [1] and d^4 in measure [4] above for instance, are indispensable to the performance of the *banhu,* and the grace notes of e in measures [5] through [7] are absolutely important to the performance of the *erhu.*

Next look at "Xiao Fangniu" (The Little Cowherd):

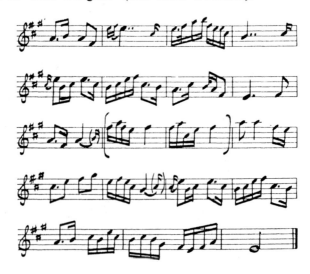

Foundations of the Chinese Orchestra

The first phrase (bars [1] and [2] is built upon the ascending fifth A-E. The next phrase, measures [3] and [4], contains a basic structure of the descending fourth, E-B. The third phrase (bars [5] and [6] cadences on the note C#, which is unstable and leads to the next phrase which ends on the most important note, E. The section following consists of three short phrases of one measure each, bars [9], [10], and [11], and terminates on an F, giving an incomplete feeling to the music. And indeed, in one vocal version of the same piece arranged by Zhang Shu (1909-1938) and titled "Lugou Wenda" (Questions and Answers at Lugou), these three measures were used to pose the beginning of a question. By following through the measures [12] to [19], one may conclude that the basis set in this passage is EABE with E as the tonic:

the unstable cadences being built upon F and C. We will mark the basis set with an asterisk and the unstable notes with crosses:

Chinese Music and Orchestration

"Liuyang River" of Hunan, as performed on the horizontal open-string zither, *zheng*, begins with the Sanban[3] passage:

If we examine closely, the arpeggiated chords employed here together with the scale passages already ascertains its Zhi tonality with the basis set:

In this investigation, we shall take the point of view that the understanding of the basis set structure in relation to modes is of value in aiding the analysis of the harmony system of a music, otherwise merely arguing about what mode a passage is written in could be a fruitless venture. As we shall see later, the basis set concept is extremely important in understanding the underlying harmony system of Chinese music. We might also stress that the basis set for any one mode may not have the same structure in different regions of China. For example, a D Yu mode may have the basis set of DGAD or DFAD. In the latter case the basis set coincides with the minor triad of Western harmony, but not in the former.

---

[3] Free tempo. Music is unmeasured.

Foundations of the Chinese Orchestra

TYPES OF ORCHESTRAS

The Chinese orchestras have the most diversified tone qualities and frequency ranges. Different orchestras belonging to different geographical regions and culture have vastly different preferences on the range of instruments. They also present an amazingly large spectrum of colorful instrumental practices. Broadly speaking, the instrumental makeup of Chinese orchestras can be divided into plucked strings, bowed strings, percussions, and winds. Table 1 presents a view of the instrumental distribution of a number of the orchestras. This Table is by no means exhaustive. In this investigation we shall analyze and study the orchestration practices which were important to the makeup of the many, purely instrumental and theatrical orchestras of China, to prepare us for the optimized usage of past experience in Chinese composition and orchestration. Even up till the present time, geographical and cultural barriers have often prevented the true appreciation of music from different stylistic schools of China and the proper interpretation of music as performed by orchestras not familiar enough with the stylistic origin of a regional music. Our investigation also aims at providing better insight to the interpretation of the many schools of orchestral music.

As we can readily observe, the Sizhu orchestras and the Chuida orchestras form the largest groups in Table 1. The Sizhu (silk and bamboo) orchestras and the Chuida (reed and percussion) orchestras practice rather different orchestrations. "Si" here refers to plucked and bowed strings, and "Zhu" refers to the bamboo winds. The Jiangnan Sizhu orchestra, one of the most popular Sizhu orchestras which originated in Jiangsu province, uses a wide range of plucked strings including the *pipa, yueqin,* small *sanxian, zheng, yangqin,* and *qinqin* (or a *zhongruan*). These plucked strings fall into several distinct categories

Chinese Music and Orchestration

Table 1. Examples of Orchestra Types

1. Silk & Bamboo School of Jiangnan (Jiangnan Sizhu)
2. Guangdong music (Cantonese music)
3. Yue Opera (Yueju) Lyrical Orchestra
4. Southern music of Fujian province
5. Pre-curtain music of Henan Ballad Singing
6. Music of Chao-zhou (Teo-chew) area
7. The Eight Suites of Shanxi province
8. Reed & Percussion School of Northern China
9. Reed & Percussion School of Zhejiang province
10. Reed & Percussion School of Southern Jiangsu province (Sunan Chuida)

INSTRUMENTS	1	2	3	4	5	6	7	8	9	10
Double Reeds:										
Suona (high)							X	X		
Suona (low)							X	X		
Suona								X	X	X
Haidi								X		
Guan							X	X		
Houguan		X								
Di (reeded flute)	X	X	X		X	X	X	X	X	X
Xiao-di								X		
Sheng	X		X		X	X	X	X	X	
Xiao	X	X	X	X		X				
Others:					Munzi					[1]

[1] Xianfeng, haotong, & zhaojun.

Foundations of the Chinese Orchestra

11. Reed & Percussion School of Chao-zhou (Teo-chew)
12. Liyuan Opera of Fujian province
13. Liuqin Opera
14. Pingju of Hebei province
15. Shanghai Opera (Huju)
16. Xi Opera (Changxi Opera)
17. Henan Bangzi Opera (Yuju)
18. Shaanxi Bangzi Opera (Qinqiang)
19. Peking Opera
20. Flower Drum Opera (Huaguxi) of Hunan province

11	12	13	14	15	16	17	18	19	20
X									
X							X	X	X
								X	
X	X						X	X	
								X	
							[7]		

---

[7] Dahao, & hailuo.

Chinese Music and Orchestration

INSTRUMENTS	\multicolumn{10}{c}{ORCHESTRA TYPE}
	1	2	3	4	5	6	7	8	9	10
Bowed String:										
Erhu	X		X		X				X	
Zhonghu	X		X							
Dahu			X							
Jinghu					X					
Banhu										
Zhuihu					X					
Yuehu		X								
Yehu	X				X					
Sihu[2]										
Maguhu[3]										
Datong										
Matouqin[4]										
Ruangong (Soft-bow)					X					
Erxian				X		X				
Sanxian						X				
Damouxian						X				
Zhuxian						X				

---

[2] Sihu is also popular in inner Mongolia and the Northeast.

[3] Maguhu is the high pitched fiddle of the Zhuang nationality of Guangxi province in Southern China.

[4] Matouqin, a bass fiddle, is a popular instrument of the Mongolian nationality.

Foundations of the Chinese Orchestra

11	12	13	14	15	16	17	18	19	20
				x	x			x	
	x		x						
								x	x
			x			x	x		
					x				
								x	
									x

Chinese Music and Orchestration

INSTRUMENTS	1	2	3	4	5	6	7	8	9	10
Plucked String:										
Yangqin (Grand Dulcimer)		X	X				X			
Liuqin										
Yueqin	X					X				
Pipa	X		X	X		X				
Sanxian	X	X	X	X	X	X			X	
Large Sanxian						X				
Piqin						X				
Huluqin						X				
Qinqin or Zhongruan	X	X				X				
Zheng	X					X	X			
Qin						X				
Se										
Percussion:										
Bo (Cymbal)							X	X	X	X
Jingbo							X	X	X	X
Luo (Gong)						X				X
Tanggu (Drum)							X		X	
Danpigu (Single membrane drum)	X		X		X					X
Xiaogu (Small drum)						X		X		X
Muyu (Wood block)						X				
Bangzi (Wood block)		X					X	X		
Paiban (Wood clappers)	X			X	X	X				
Yunluo (Gong chime)							X		X	X
Others				Ling bang		Xiang-zhan	5		Cibo	6

---

[5] Muban (clapper), zhegu (drum), guoshan ban (clapper), gujiao bo (cymbal), Shuangguan, kangluo (gong), huabo (cymbal), yinqing, ling (bell), qing.

[6] Hailuo (shell horn).

Foundations of the Chinese Orchestra

```
11   12   13   14   15   16   17   18   19   20


              X
                                      X    X
         X
         X

X



X    X                                X
X    X                                X
X    X                                X
     X                                X
     X                                X
X

                              X    X
X                                     X
8    9
```

---

[8] Gouzi luo (gong), shenbo (cymbal), qingzi, zhonggu (drum), kangluo (gong)

[9] Large pai, small pai, guban, wanluo (gong), small jiao, gubian luo (gong), niuzhan, liangzhan, shuangling (double bell), du.

Chinese Music and Orchestration

as far as performance techniques and tone qualities go. The *zheng* and the *yangqin* are open-stringed instruments (for the range and tuning of the principal plucked strings, refer to Lee Yuan-yuan [Lee, 1979]). The *zheng* is performed with fingernails and the *yangqin* is performed with a pair of "Zhu" (bamboo hammers). The *pipa, yueqin, qinqin, ruan* and *sanxian* belong to the "Tantiao" system. Their performance techniques are based heavily on the fundamental action of "Tan," playing with the index finger to the left or downward, the "Tiao," plucking the string with the thumb upward or to the right. *Sanxian* differs from the rest of the members of the "Tantiao" family, especially in left-hand techniques. It is not a fretted plucked string and a different variety of manipulation of the tone is possible on the *sanxian*. The plucked strings have a long history of ensemble cooperation. Let us look at the traditional partnership of *pipa* and *sanxian* in "Tanci" for example.

"Tanci" of the Jiangsu province is a well-known style of music in which recitative singing is accompanied by instruments. In the Qing dynasty, the principle instruments used in "Tanci" was already *sanxian* and *pipa*, with the occasional addition of *yangqin*. Today, when only one instrument is used, it is most likely the *sanxian*. When two instruments are used, the traditional partners *sanxian* and *pipa* are played by a male performer and a female performer respectively, the upper part of the melody being performed on the *sanxian* (small *sanxian*) and the lower part on the *pipa*. In a joint venture of "Hui Shu," several *pipa*'s, several *sanxian*'s, the *qinqin* and the *erhu* are used.

An example of the music of the traditional partners, *sanxian* and *pipa*, selected from "Zhenzhu Ta" (the Pearl Tower) as sung by Hou Jiu-xia and notated by Ge Tang (Jiangsu, 1955), is shown below.

Foundations of the Chinese Orchestra

As researchers of orchestral music well know, the correct blending of even two instruments takes many years and decades of experimentation. The orchestral structure of all of the orchestras in Table 1 are based on long-term partnership of the instruments. Partners since the 16th century used in "Kunqu," including the di, *xiao, sheng, pipa, guan, sanxian* and so on, probably have the greatest influence on the Sizhu orchestras.

The Chuida orchestras vary widely in composition. Various sizes and types of *suona* (double reed conical wind) and *guan* (cylindrical reed pipe) are the lead instruments in many of the Chuida orchestras. Sunan Chuida orchestra of Southern Jiangsu, however, emphasizes more on the *di*. The pitch characteristics of the percussions varies drastically from one orchestra to another. But within one orchestra, only very narrow pitch variations for any one percussive instrument is allowed. Otherwise the percussions simply do not blend correctly and unwanted effects may result.

Chinese Music and Orchestration

Today popular instruments such as *pipa, ruan, zheng, erhu, zhonghu, dahu* (or *gehu*), *dihu* (or *beigehu*), *di, sheng, suona, houguan*, etc. have been consistently absorbed into orchestras which were originally more localized. One example is the Yuju (Henan Bangzi) orchestra which originally consisted of *piaohu* (*Yuju banhu*, alto-ranged), *erhu, sanxian, sheng, di, luo, gu, cha, bangzi*. etc. is now expanded to include all of the above instruments (Liu, 1979) which are popular all over China. The trend of the local orchestras is definitely towards expansion in instrumentation.

The flourishing of regional music-drama which continued through the centuries since the Song dynasty (960-1279) until the present day has created a large number of theatrical orchestras. Musically, they vary tremendously in style and instrumentation. The Yue opera (Yueju) orchestra, Pingju orchestra, Peking opera (Jingju) orchestra, etc. in Table 1 belong to this category. Bowed strings, the *huqin*'s, play very important roles in their orchestration. We will analyze their music at a later stage. The Liyuan Opera orchestra, however, does not use bowed-strings as the lead instrument.

The Liyuan Opera orchestra of Fujian is a highly sophisticated orchestra in Southern China. Its principal instrumentation employs *dongxiao* (vertical flute) as the key wind and *pipa* as the key plucked-string. The string, wind, and percussion division is as follows:

String: *pipa, sanxian, zhonghu* (or large *erhu*)

Wind: *dongxiao, pinxiao (di), da-ai* (large *suona*), *xiao-ai* (small *suona*)

Percussion: *tanggu, paigu* (small drum), *dapai, xiao pai, guban* (four pieces of pillow-shaped wood), *daluo, xiaoluo* (medium *tangluo*), *wanluo* (bowl-*gong*, or small *tangluo*), *xiaojiao* (also known as *goujiao*, another small *tangluo*) *gubianluo, niuzhan, liangzhan* (also known as *shuangyin*,

Foundations of the Chinese Orchestra

larger than *niuzhan*, the pair of *zhan*'s are brought to contact when played), *shuangling, dabo, xiaobo, du.*

Among the wind instrument, *dongxiao* and *di* are seldom used together, the reason being incompatibility in tone quality. The percussion section is led by the *tanggu*, unlike the case of Peking opera where the *danpigu* (small high-pitched single-membraned drum) leads the percussions. The *paigu* (small drum) in the Liyuan Opera orchestra is only used when the music tenses up. We note here that the geometry of the *paigu* is closer to the small drums used by Kunqu orchestras and Yiyang styled orchestras. The inner diameter of the membrane is larger than that used by Peking Opera orchestras. The performance of the *tanggu* is complemented by the *xiaoluo* (the medium *tangluo*, as in puppet theaters of Southern Fujian). The rhythmic pattern and dynamic effect of the *tanggu, xiaoluo* and *paigu* performance suggest a close relation between Liyuan Opera music and the Yiyang style. Like in a number of other popular theatrical music, the ending phrase of a melodic section is often divided into two parts sung in harmony (Huadong, 1955).

THE USE OF THE STRINGS

The Chinese tradition of using strings in the orchestra is quite different from practices of the European or the American tradition. In a large majority of instrumental orchestras, as opposed to the theatrical orchestras, the plucked strings have assumed a leading role in orchestration over the bowed strings, for the very reason that the Chinese plucked strings have such a long standing history of popularity, and musical development.

The theatrical orchestras, which became popular during the last five hundred years or so, often employ a lead bowed-string. Excellent

Chinese Music and Orchestration

examples are the *erhu* in Huju, *jinghu* in Peking opera, alto *banhu* in Yuju, *banhu* in Qinqiang, *zhuihu* in Quju, *zhonghu* in Yueju, *touxian* in Chaoju, and so on. Qi Ru-shan made a very interesting observation (Qi, 1949): In Peking opera, the *yueqin* traditionally played an extremely important part. When the *jinghu* performed a long and extended note, the *yueqin* would always take over with its lunzhi, creating a dramatic orchestrational effect. For some reason, the *yueqin* was later de-emphasized and its performance was so deteriorated that only one string of the *yueqin* was used anymore in Peking opera, and the fingernail techniques were replaced by one of plectrum. It was probably a result of both the over-emphasis of bowed strings, and the shrinkage of theatrical orchestras due to economic decline. In any case, the Chinese experience indicates that the plucked strings are at least as important as the bowed strings in an orchestra, if not more important. There is a slight tendency these day of a decline in the ability to use plucked strings in their well-experienced roles. But more experienced composers seldom fall into that trap.

THE SANXIAN'S

Statistically speaking, *sanxian* is probably the most utilized instrument of the many types of orchestras of China (see Table 1). *Sanxian* differs from other members of the plucked string family in that it is an instrument utilizing the resonance of a skin membrane whereas *pipa*, *liuqin*, *ruan*, *yangqin*, *zheng*, *yueqin* and so on utilize the resonance of a wooden sounding board. *Sanxian* probably have the longest history of popularity among the masses compared with the other plucked strings. The small *sanxian* of Jiangnan has a small drum (drum is the name by which *sanxian's* python skin-covered resonator is known. It may be related to the fact that the resonator is acoustically a drum, and the

Foundations of the Chinese Orchestra

ancestor of *sanxian* as a drum, *xiantao*) and its characteristic tonal quality is that generated by a string under relatively high tension over a resonator covered with a thin skin, sometimes percussive. The combined effect of the string and the small drum is rich in higher harmonics and its performance is highly ornamental, a typical example being offered by the beginning section of "The Past and the Present" (Jin Xi) performed by the Shanghai Minzu Yuetuan (Shanghai Traditional Orchestra) as shown.

The effect of tonal manipulation of the small *sanxian* arouses musical interest of an unpredictable kind (China Record, M-513). *Sanxian* is a

Chinese Music and Orchestration

fretless instrument. The characteristic gliding embellishments on some of the modally distinguished notes creates immense overtones which form an important contribution to orchestral effects. In the above example from "The Past and the Present" the *sanxian* was not present, and the above orchestrational effect was lost. Effects of small *sanxian* of the distinctly Jiangnan or other Southern character can also be found in such outstanding orchestra work of the silk and bamboo school as "Wedding Processional" (Xing Jie), 'Zhonghua Liuban" (the most embellished orchestral version of Lao Liuban, Lai, 1979) performed by the Shanghai Traditional Orchestra (China Record M-032). The musical role played by the large *sanxian* in the Chinese orchestra is very different from that of the small *sanxian*. Its tonal quality is one that gives a feeling of a string-membrane coupled system with the string under low tension. It has a large drum almost 9 inches along the long axis and offers a full and deep voice. A dynamic performance on the large *sanxian*, selected from "Days of Emancipation" (Fanshen De Rizi) performed by the Xinying Traditional Orchestra, is shown below.

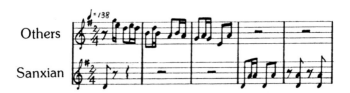

The roles of the small and the large *sanxian* are really quite different: the small is acoustically manipulative and thus arouses excitement, and the large has low and stable voices and long reverberation. These effects make them both important in orchestration.

Foundations of the Chinese Orchestra

YANGQIN

Yangqin in Jiangnan Sizhu and Guangdong music (Cantonese music) carries the most intricately ornamented melody and ascertains the harmonic bases of the music. To get a feeling of the kind of sophisticated musical performance we are talking about, one may examine any passage from "Wedding Processional" (for example, see below). The octave doubling harmonically important is know as "chen yin", and they are marked with an asterisk in the examples. The performance is highly improvisational; The player reacts to the environment in which he or she plays, in particular to whom he or she is playing with. The degree of ornamentation is a function of time and place and ensemble partner.

Yangqin part in "Wedding Processional".

Chinese Music and Orchestration

The popular "Rain Falls on the Plantains" (Yu Da Bajiao) is a good example of the Guangdong styled role of *yangqin* (see below). The orchestrational effect of *yangqin* in Jiangnan Sizhu and Cantonese music are similar in many respects, with the *yangqin* in "Rain Falls on the Plantains".

Example of the lead role of *yangqin* in "Rain Falls on the Plantains".

The versatility in the performing techniques of *yangqin*, employing a large number of combinations of wrist and finger actions, and the wide frequency range of four to five octaves, makes *yangqin* an indispensable member of the Chinese orchestra. The noted conductor, Zhen Xun, of the Zhong-Guang (Central Broadcasting) Traditional Orchestra once remarked that the *yangqin* and the *sheng* are so important to Chinese

Foundations of the Chinese Orchestra

orchestration that one must have them before one has anything else. That statement is really not an exaggeration. The hammers of *yangqin* are a pair of specially designed bamboo strikers whose hammering surfaces are covered with thin leather. The performance of the *yangqin* can be controlled so that within a passage, certain notes can be made muffed and others crisp and bright. We illustrate this point by referring the reader to the *yangqin* passage selected from "Fishing Song of the East China Sea" by Ma Shenglong and Gu Guanren, performed by the Shanghai Traditional Orchestra with the maestro He Wu-qi conducting.

SHENG

A name for the *sheng* documented 15th century BC on oracle bones was *"he"*, or "harmony". The use of *sheng* in the orchestra is a practice at least three thousand years old, and indeed the coupled vibration of the pipe and free reed has the effect of blending, or harmonizing other instruments whose overtone structure present obvious tonal gaps. In the northern styled orchestras, where double-reeds such as *haidi, suona* and *guan* are the key instruments, the *sheng* is an indispensable accompanying instrument. The Jiangnan styled orchestras have had a long history of orchestral practice, which employs the *sheng* for harmonizing the plucked strings, the bowed strings and other bamboo winds.

Chinese Music and Orchestration

The harmonies performed on the *sheng* is designed so that the differences in volume among the members of a chord is utilized to characterize the tonality of the music. We show an example of chords for the heptatonic scale steps beginning with D_5.

Examples of chords performed on the *sheng* to
illustrate the note-doubling procedure.

The deliberate doubling of important notes are illustrated. On the other hand, the same principle of loudness contrast is also used to build chords which perform the function of special effects, sometimes disharmonizing. The example below performed by Hu Tian-quan is one in which the small notes of A_4, B_4-sharp, and C_5 (actually softer note when performed) are used to decorate the D_6 in *fortissimo*.

The *sheng* is not just an accompanying instrument, or one that produces only special effects. Its transparent and sweet voice, when used to play Chinese harmonies, produces a mellow and full sound. The *sheng* in solo passages creates a distinctly Chinese atmosphere. We illustrates the use of *sheng* in describing "the ocean at dawn" in *sanban* (free tempo), chosen from "Fishing Song of the East China Sea" by Ma

Foundations of the Chinese Orchestra

Shenglong and Gu Guanren as performed by the Shanghai Traditional Orchestra. This phrase on the *zhongyin sheng* (middle-register *sheng*) is

The role of *sheng* in section one, The ocean at dawn, from "Fishing Song of the East China Sea".

followed by a phrase of identical structure with a pitch center an octave higher on the *gaoyin sheng* (high-register *sheng*). This practice creates both register and tonal contrasts, and is often done. Below is a *sheng* solo passage, accompanied by a duet of *di's*, from "the Dance of Yao" by Liu Tie-shan, Mao Yuan and Peng Xiu-wen. Here the combined effect of the *sheng* and the *di's*, providing higher harmonics simulates the

Chinese Music and Orchestration

south-western styled *lusheng* performance. However, it is important that the volume of the *di*'s does not overshadow the *sheng*.

The number of sounding pipes, called *miao*, in the *sheng* has gone through many changes during the course of history. The ancient *yu* for instance, had over thirty *miao's* (mostly thirty six). The Jiangnan styled *sheng*, also known as *Susheng*, have seventeen *miao's*. In today's traditional orchestras, the number of *miao's* has returned to about thirty six (Fang, 1978). The typical range of the high-register and the middle-register *sheng* are shown respectively below (Liu, 1978).

Compass of the high-register *sheng*. The range in parenthesis is extension beyond the most widely used range.

Compass of the middle-register *sheng*

Foundations of the Chinese Orchestra

THE DOUBLE REEDS

The Chinese double-reeds offer a complete continuum in frequency range and tonal quality. The popular *haidi's* have A_4 or B_4 as their fundamental tone and span a compass of two octaves all the way into B_6. The *suona's* occupy a complete range of fundamental tones of $G4$ to A_2, with a high of G_6. The *haidi's* and *suona's* are near-conical resonators, and their low register range is joined both in pitch and in tonal quality of the large diameter *guan's* which are straight cylinders, forming the bass group of the double-reed family, with another group of *houguan's*, which are small diameter straight cylinders with a horn, covering the common range of the medium register. The popular *houguan's* have fundamental pitches ranging from G_3 to A_2, and the large *guan's* have fundamental tones from G_4 to G_3 (three popular ones have compasses G_4-A_6, D_4-E_6, and G_3-C_6). The geometrical construction of the double-reeds, as schematically shown below, makes use of several acoustic properties of pipes. First, the highest of the group, the *haidi's* and the *suona's* are conical. As we know, for the same length of pipe, a perfect cone has a fundamental tone an octave higher than the straight cylinder. Then the *houguan's* are small cylinders with a horn which tends to raise its lower frequencies, thus filling the middle continuum. The bass range are ideally occupied by the large straight cylinders, *guan's*.

This double-reed family from cones to cylinders forms an integral part of the Chinese orchestra in its chuida wing. The "Overture" (Xu Qu) of the dance drama "The Dagger Society" (Xiao Dao Hui) composed by Shang Yi and performed by the Shanghai Opera's Traditional Orchestra uses the bass *guan* for its powerful beginning passage. In the middle register between A_2 and E_5, if the shrill tone of the cones (*suona's*) is not desired, one switches to *houguan*. For example, "The Dance of Yao" uses an F-*houguan*. The traditional performance of these double-reeds offer tremendous tonal interest in their embellishments and

Chinese Music and Orchestration

offer qualities important to the intensity and warmth of the orchestral effect.

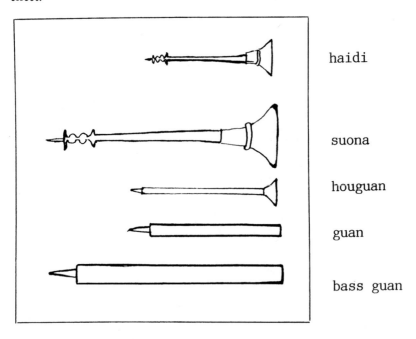

Pipe shapes employed in the acoustical design of the Chinese double-reed family.

Beginning passage from "Overture" to the dance drama "the Dagger Society".

Foundations of the Chinese Orchestra

The F-*houguan* performing the first dance theme in "the Dance of Yao".

the D-*houguan* in "The Dance of Yao". *Heng-xiao* is the horizontal *xiao* (without the reed membrane of the *di)*.

REFERENCES

Fang, Pu-dong, private communication (1978).

Huadong Xiqu Yanjiuyuan (Institute for Theatrical Music of Eastern China), *Huadong Xiqu Juzhong Jieshao* (Introduction to the Types of Theatrical Styles of Eastern China), Xin Wenyi Chubanshe (New Literature and Arts Publisher), Shanghai (1955).

Chinese Music and Orchestration

Jiangsu Nanbu Minjian Xiqu Shuochang Yinyue Ji (A Collection of Theatrical and Ballad Singing Music of Southern Jiangsu), edited by the Committee on Music Research of the Jiangsu Province, Yinyue Chubanshe (Music Publisher), Beijing (1955).

Lai, Chun-yue, "Lao Liuban," *Chinese Music*, Vol. 2, No. 4, p. 47 (1979).

Lee, Yuan-yuan, "The Liuye-Qin and Wang Huiran," *Chinese Music*, Vol. 2, No. 2, p. 6 (1979).

Liu, Wen-jin, private communication (1978).

Liu, Wen-jin, private communication (1979).

Qi, Ru-shan, *Guoju Yishu Huikao* (1949).

The Acoustical Space of the Chinese Orchestra

ON THE ACOUSTICAL SPACE OF THE CHINESE ORCHESTRA[4]

The acoustical makeup of the Chinese orchestra is analyzed, and the fundamental tonal spectrum groups identified. It is found that compared with the Western symphony which has one fundamental spectrum group - the violin group - the Chinese orchestra has two fundamental spectrum groups - that of the sheng-guan (reeded winds dominated by free reeds) and that of the tan-bo (plucked strings). The acoustical space of the Chinese orchestra is thus richer than that of the Western symphony. The roles of the special color instruments, in particular the erhu vertical fiddle and the percussions, are discussed in detail. This paper is a must for all composers.

INTRODUCTION

This paper is based on a lecture given at the International Conference on Chinese Music, Beijing, China, August-September, 1988. We discuss the makeup of the fundamental tonal spectrum of the Chinese

---

[4] Originally published in *Chinese Music*, Vol. 11, No. 4 (1988). Chinese version was published in *People's Music*, No. 2 of year 1989.

Chinese Music and Orchestration

orchestra from both an acoustical as well as an artistic angle. Many of our conclusions support the traditional use of tonal components in the regional and historical Chinese orchestras. We further discuss the role of the interval in the musical language of China, and the role of natural intervals as standards for the acoustical space of musical compositions. The inspiration for writing this paper comes from all existing compositions, old and new. I therefore thank all of our composers throughout history.

THE ORCHESTRA'S TONAL SPECTRUM AND ITS ARTISTIC UTILIZATION

There are several dozen major Chinese orchestras now known. They differ in orchestration methods and in artistic techniques. To the musicians of today and the modern musical stage, the paramount question has been the intelligent utilization of several hundred instruments in the chui (reeded winds), da (percussions), tan (plucked strings), and la (bowed strings) categories of performance technique. How do we maximize their power together and how do we maximize the level of artistic sensitivity that compositions utilizing them can provide.

Concerning the orchestration emphasis of the regional orchestras, I have touched upon in my series of papers on the foundation of the Chinese orchestra published in Chinese Music. Each one of those orchestras can be recognized as a prototype for extensive practical utilization. In this paper we do not restrict ourselves to any one geographical region. We will study from the angle of orchestra acoustics, we will study the acceptance to the audience of orchestral art, and we will discuss and deduce the appropriate composition mentality for writing orchestral work.

The Acoustical Space of the Chinese Orchestra

The first concept I will discuss is the fundamental tonal spectrum of an orchestra. An orchestra is vastly different from an instrument. An instrument has a frequency spectrum, representing a distinctive range of tone. Some instruments have tones of a similar type throughout its range. For example, the violin and the liuqin both have a wide compass and the tonal quality of each does change from the high register, through the middle register, to the low register, but the basic tone quality throughout the compass is of the same type. The same is true of the banhu, another instrument based on wood plate vibration as the violin and the liuqin. Other instruments such as the erhu or the saxophone are quite different from the group we just discussed in that they project a vastly different personality at different ranges: the tonal quality at different register are of different types. To the instrumental composer, both types of instruments are easy to grasp. But when it comes to orchestration the situation is vastly different.

The European symphony is a more recent product of mankind. Its orchestral spectrum is quite a bit simpler than that of the Chinese orchestra and is therefore better understood. It utilizes a basic tonal spectrum of the violin family. All other instrumental spectra present are not fundamental to the orchestra's orchestration and are supplementary. These other spectra are used for special color and function in contrast with the fundamental spectrum of the violin family. The sound of the symphony orchestra when it comes through our perception is that of the violin group.

The Chinese orchestra also has both types of spectra, fundamental versus supplementary. But because of the extraordinarily extensive period of practice, the Chinese orchestra possesses an extraordinary range of resonators and acoustical materials. Its fundamental tone thus can have several possibilities. Broadly speaking, the Chinese orchestra has two groups of fundamental tones, and the Western symphony has one.

Chinese Music and Orchestration

Many of our twentieth century compositions for the Chinese orchestra mistakenly used the huqin vertical fiddle group as the fundamental spectra. This is contrary to acoustical understanding. We have witnessed in practice that when the 'huqin group' is used as the fundamental spectrum for composition, its power is rather limited, and the benefit cost ratio is low.

What makes a fundament spectrum and what makes a special color spectrum are decided by the intimate relation between the spectral characteristics and the musical psychology of the audience. For some instruments, solo use is more powerful standing against a fundamental orchestral spectrum, but when used in group the tone becomes muddy. Other spectrum can be extremely powerful, easily controlled in spectral width, and highly flexible in texture. This is particularly true of the tanbo (tanbo) - plucked string family, the sheng-guan (shengguan) - reeded wind family of China and the violin family of Europe.

What is the foundation of the fundamental tones of the Chinese orchestra in terms of acoustics and musical psychology?

First Fundamental Spectrum - the Shengguan

Probably the most important but often unnoticed group is the shengguanyue. This group has the incredible ability to grow and shrink in tonal breadth, and can be easily utilized for fundamental orchestral spectrum. Here the two terms 'sheng' and 'guan' represent a full range of coupled resonators: free reeds and air-column in resonators, membrane and air-column in resonators, and pressured reeds and air-column in resonators. By itself the shengguanyue is a complete orchestra - it possesses all the quality to make an orchestra. This quality can only be judged with acoustical and musical psychology standards. The nomenclature used here departs from the traditional use of the term shengguan. Shengguanyue is used to represent the most important tonal

The Acoustical Space of the Chinese Orchestra

spectrum - the shengguan spectrum of the Chinese orchestra. This spectrum consists of

- the shrill tone of the pressured small reed,
- the full-bodied tone of the coupled air-column, and
- the full harmonies from the resonance of free-reed and air-column.

Decades ago the Chinese music community became enthralled with the tonal capability of the lusheng orchestra of Southwestern China. The musical interest offered by the lusheng orchestra is but a subset of the musical interest of the shengguan group. But from the interest in the lusheng orchestra one can imagine the power of the shengguan spectrum.

The high, middle and low register sheng's (free-reed mouth organs) and the bawu (free-reed flute) provided rounded smooth tones characteristic of free reeds coupled to air columns. Here the bawu utilizes a single reed at different angles for coupling to a large range of air columns. As a result the dynamic range systematically decreases towards the high notes. This must be taken into account when the bawu is used in the orchestra. The combination of the sheng and pressured reeds (the sheng and the guan, the sheng and the suona and the haidi, for example) has been used in a large number of traditional orchestral experiences. The low-register houguan (bass double-reed cylindrical air-column) comes in handy for low-range support.

It should be pointed out that the shengguan group is often torn apart today in compositions. Loud combinations of suona, when unsupported by the di (reeded flute) and the sheng group, are monotonous. This technique can be utilized when the balance of dynamics is fully realized in the dynamics space of the composition envisioned by the composer.

Chinese Music and Orchestration

Membrane and air column make up the tone of the di, which moisten the high frequencies of the pressured reed. This method is useful. Solo di passages, and di duets in thirds and fourths heard frequently in recent decades are not effective. Traditional use of the sheng and di combination has its acoustical reasons.

Second Fundamental Spectrum - the Tanbo

The second fundamental Chinese orchestral spectrum is tanboyue, or plucked strings. It is well known that the plucked string orchestra of China is the most complete in the world. It is complete in several ways, but most importantly in the compliments of resonator types, acoustical material and performance techniques. The resonator types and acoustical materials used are not haphazard, but have been developed for orchestral group use over the centuries. On top of that, performance techniques most highly developed allow a vast number of tone patterns to be used by composers of the plucked-string orchestra music. As a result the plucked string orchestral group possesses the powerful capabilities of tonal contrast, dynamic contrast and textural contrast.

What we are discussing here is the function of plucked strings as a fundamental tonal spectrum for the orchestra. This is a much broader use in concept than what is represented by the plucked string ensemble used in pieces like "Three Six" or "The Camel Bells." In those compositions the plucked strings were treated almost strictly as individual tones to be exploited and as components of a multi-part harmony. Those are simplistic uses. One should look at the breadth of the harmonic content in this fundamental spectrum and treat it as an orchestral texture capable of growing and shrinking.

Let us examine what makes this group so versatile. This branch of the Chinese orchestra is unusually rich in tonal quality. It encompasses:

The Acoustical Space of the Chinese Orchestra

- high-frequency range plate resonators excited by tantiao plucked performance,
- low-frequency range plate resonator excited by tantiao plucked performance,
- middle to low frequency range membrane resonator excited by tantiao plucked performance,
- broad frequency range plate/box resonator excited by jixuan struck performance,
- low range long resonator/long string open-string excitation, and
- low and broad range long resonator/long string fingerboard excitation.

The extent of spectral versatility of this component is no less than that of the shengguanyue. The combination and organic utilization of both groups are unmatched anywhere.

The more commonly used cooperative spectrum from this group evokes specific musical interest and musical psychology. The high to middle range cooperative spectrum involving the liuqin (high-range curved-back plucked lute), the yangqin (the grand hammered dulcimer), and the pipa (the curve-backed grand lute) spans a range of effects to the audience. It can provide a wide range from cold and dry sound to somewhat heated sound, but the real warmth does not begin to be detected until the zhongruan (the mid to low range flat-back round lute) joins in. This is ironical. The sanxian (the bass long-stringed membrane-resonator lute), the zheng (the open-stringed zither with a large and long resonator providing a broad range of tones from low to high), the se (the even-larger open-string zither with a long resonator), and the daruan (the bass flat-backed round lute) provide a whole range of powerful low frequency for outlining harmonic or melodic skeleton in compositions, and for mood setting. Strong characters in different ranges

Chinese Music and Orchestration

can be handled forcefully with the liuqin and the sanxian when their tones become associated with specific characters. Moving and unstable musical motives are more easily handled with the qin (the unique instrument offering five octaves of open-string, full-stopped, and harmonics tones), the zheng, and the se.

The practice of using the tanbo tonal spectrum as fundamental to the orchestra is reasonably popular, but the practice can certainly be improved several fold. A good example is offered by the use of plucked strings as a fundamental tonal spectrum by Liu Wen-jin in "The Unforgettable Water-Splashing Festival." Several movements of that piece truly show the power of the spectrally versatile tanbo group. Ma Shenglong and Gu Guanren in "Fishing Song of the East China Sea" used this group successfully in rhythmic functions as a group. But it can be said that it was a more limited use compared with what this group offers acoustically and in terms of evocable musical psychology.

The spectrum of the tanbo group and that of the western symphony (the violin group) are easily combined. This is of interest to composers writing for the symphony category. From the angle of psychology, the plucked string group enhances the power of the violin group with its tonal spectrum (both a result of the wave form and the attacks offered by the performance techniques). If we can just improve on the use of the shengguan group, the complementarity between the shengguan and the tanbo is more than natural.

The tantiao family of pipa, liuqin and other have acoustical radiation on stage of the dipolar type. This means it makes no difference whether they are placed on the left side or the right side of the stage. On the other hand, if they are placed in the middle facing the audience, the effects are weakest. Problems such as these do not require large amounts of experiments to solve because the theory and common sense already exist.

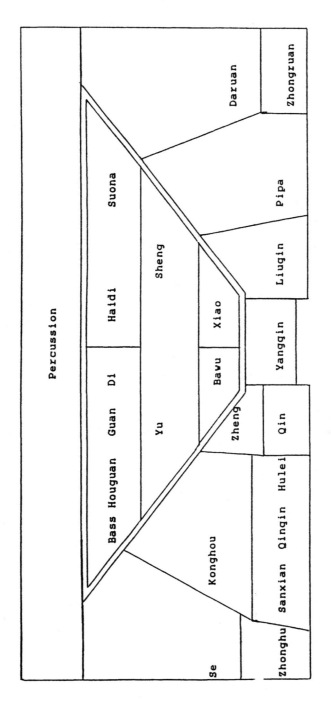

Fig. 1. The acoustical marriage of the shengguan spectrum and the tanbo spectrum. Special color instruments including the zhuihu, the erhu and the banhu can be placed in front with the bawu, the xiao and the yangqin.

Chinese Music and Orchestration

Considerations for the Special Colors

Having proposed the fundamental tonal spectrum for the Chinese orchestra we will discuss the role of the other instruments as special color instruments.

The huqin vertical fiddles are fabulous instruments as we all know, but acoustically they are not the group to be used as a fundamental spectral group. The popular solo erhu has unbelievable penetrating power in the orchestra. They also have their power in a group. But from the angle of orchestral efficiency, the erhu group is better accompanied than serving as fundamental tonal spectrum of an orchestra. In a concert hall the ear can tract pitch, tone color and dynamic nuances of instrumental tones with speed and precision. It has been recognized that the ear is most effective with tones consisting of specific harmonic makeup. The ear reacts favorably to the solo erhu spectrum but less so to an ensemble erhu spectrum. The same is true of the zhonghu, the mid-range erhu, and the dahu, the low-range huqin. This phenomenon has to do with the relative strength of the lower partials with respect to the upper, and the pattern in which the upper partials fall off. In terms of orchestral acoustics, the huqin (especially the membrane-resonator huqin) does not perform in the fundamental tonal spectrum role compared with the solo (or duet) role. On the other hand, the shengguan and the tanbo groups do an outstanding job as orchestral basis as far as the ear is concerned. The same is true of the violin group. The reasons are strictly one of musical psychology that is driven by acoustics.

These considerations have widespread implications. The acoustic angle directly affects the analysis of musical psychology before any cultural filtering enters in. These considerations allow orchestras to be designed with a high benefit-to-cost ratio.

The Acoustical Space of the Chinese Orchestra

Having said that the huqin group did not qualify for a fundamental orchestral spectrum, I must say that the erhu group in terms of an erhu ensemble (not in an orchestra) has tremendous potential. The format of erhu ensemble (in unison or in duet) as in "Wave after Wave of Golden Wheat" (Wang Guotong and Li Xiuqi) has its artistic appeal. The erhu group singing the South-of-Yangzi styled passage in "Fishing Song of the East China Sea" (Ma Shenglong and Gu Guanren) can never be forgotten. These are examples of excellent use of the erhu group without subjecting them to the task of orchestral basis. The erhu solo in "Longhua Pagoda" (He Zhanhao) in the most depictive passage is also acoustically valid with a Western orchestral basis.

The percussion music of China as a separate musical entity has established itself artistically beyond any doubt. Its status is unmatched by the percussion music of the Western genre. The artistic success of the Chinese percussion music hinges on several crucial features. First, it is a living ensemble. From the South to the North, and from the West to the East, Chinese percussion music is always played in an ensemble. In most instances, the ensemble depends on a few critical instruments. These instruments are so critical to the ensemble that the ensemble is handicapped without any one of them. These whole combinations probably achieve the highest level in conceptual flexibility. This high degree of flexibility and creativity surpasses the achievements of the shengguan group or the tanbo group. This creativity of the percussion group was attained in history and to a large degree preserved in the living music today. We must not in our orchestral composition suppress or limit this creativity, and we should become inspired by this musical and acoustical creativity in our treatment of the shengguan and the tanbo - fundamental tonal spectrum - groups. The paigu as a melodic and rhythmic soloist is highly attractive, but a successful orchestral composition should not be dependent solely on a paigu solo or the support of limited segments of folk percussion oral patterns. Secondly,

Chinese Music and Orchestration

Chinese percussion music has its definite philosophy on pitch space. The development of the shengguan music and the tanbo music can be inspired by this pitch space concept, and capitalize on the magnitude of change, the rhythmic breadth, and the emphasis on the use of the sub-spaces. The predictable changes in pitch space of the xiaoluo which glides upward and the daluo which glides downward are excellent examples of this systematic concept. It is this systematic concept which we can utilize in the union of the shengguan, tanbo, and percussion groups.

In this system we place the yangqin, the bawu, and the xiao in the front center of the stage. The bawu and the xiao being directly behind the yangqin in the first row of the shengguan group which occupies the center quadrant of the stage, with the percussion directly behind the shengguan group in the same quadrant. The shengguan instruments are arranged as follows: yu and sheng are directly behind the bawu and the xiao. Here the yu performs more melodic functions and the sheng performs more harmonic function among the free-reeded mouth organs. The last row of the shengguan group consists of the bass houguan, the guan, the di, the haidi and the suona.

To the left of the stage are the tanbo with movable pitch and to the right of the stage are the tanbo of primarily the pipa family. The front row of the left group are the qin, the python-skin hulei, the python-skin qinqin, the sanxian and the zhonghu. The second row of the left group are the zheng, the konghou, and the bass se.

To the right of the stage we place the liuqin, the pipa, the zhongruan and the daruan.

THE LANGUAGE OF THE MUSIC

The pitch combinations in our compositions are not the source of our musical space. In Chinese culture, the musical space is decided by

The Acoustical Space of the Chinese Orchestra

specific measures. The relationship between points in the space possess special meanings. This includes a cultural meaning, and a compositional meaning. The language here is determined by musical intervals. The musical space can be divided several ways, but the Chinese way of interval language is one that transcends scale. This is why analyzing Chinese music using a scale approach always meets with failure. We encounter the same problem in writing Chinese orchestral music. If our musical thinking becomes one of scale, we lose sensitivity for the energy of change contained in our musical language.

Let us look at a common problem. Are octaves equal? In many compositions, it is obvious that octaves are equal in the musical space of the composer. In reality, this is an oversimplification of our thought. From the larger compositions like "Meihua Sannong" to the nice and short "New Year's Eve," the octaves are unequal. The octaves of yu-yu, zhi-zhi in "Meihua Sannong" and the gong-gong, shang-shang of "New Year's Eve," a different space is extracted. We see numerous ensemble versions of "Meihua Sannong" which alters completely the broad octave space of the musical language. This occurs in the ensemble arrangement. The musical space is all of a sudden compressed, the musical interest killed. "New Year's Eve" is a composition for the solo erhu. The ensemble arrangements for the Western string orchestra did not further the musical language. Some yangqin accompaniments also confused the complementarity of the two instruments and their spatial contrast. Further, the emphasis and balance of harmonic and melodic intervals are often neglected.

Interval dominates our musical language. This is particularly true of Chinese music. In many text books of music, the first concept introduced is that of the scale. This is highly inappropriate in view of the importance of the musical intervals over scale in Chinese music. In fact the new direction of music today is towards broadening the musical space available to us and the logical expansion is one built on intervals.

Chinese Music and Orchestration

The intervals are much more fundamental building blocks of music than scale. Further, since the intervals dominate our musical language, the temperaments directly control the balance between physical harmony and artistry. In recent centuries, the European musicians emphasized the equal temperament system, but it is a small blip in the music history of mankind. In reality the use of the equal temperament system is a simplification of our musical space. It has become monotonous and artistically limited in the subconscious realm of our brains. Composers for the Chinese orchestra must pay attention to this point - effectively utilize natural intervals and the incredible experience of a very broad tonal spectral system. The technique of resonant counterpoint under concert hall reverberation with equal-tempered intervals and natural intervals is also effective. The natural intervals of Wang Guotong and the equal-tempered intervals of Zhou Guangren in the resonance of "Fantasy on the Sanmen Gorge" (Liu Wen-jin) produced precisely this effect.

CONCLUSION

We have analyzed the roles of the shengguan and the tanbo groups as fundamental tonal spectrum instruments for the Chinese orchestra. They have used in those roles in an incredible number of Chinese orchestras from historical times to the present. And yet in the confusion of modern times we tend to ignore their natural roles. From the standpoint of concert-hall acoustics, they once again stand out, in a room-averaged fashion, as the most usable fundamental tonal spectrum instruments for the Chinese orchestra. We show in Fig. 1 a combination utilizing the two groups with the shengguan group enclosed in the middle fan space. Here the yangqin, the liuqin, the pipa, the zhongruan and the daruan belong to high, middle, and low range of plate vibration

The Acoustical Space of the Chinese Orchestra

resonators. The zheng, the qin, the se, and the konghou belong to long-stringed middle-and low-ranged plate resonators with movable-pitch performing techniques. (Their special position is due to these characteristic performance methods which allow the performance of highly unstable musical motives). The python-skin hulei, the python-skin qinqin, the sanxian and the zhonghu all belong to low- and middle-ranged membrane resonators.

Characteristic instruments for solo or small group use including the zhuihu, the jinghu, the erhu, the banhu, or even the gaohu (the acoustical data on the gaohu indicates that this is a member of the huqin family that is usable in a fundamental tonal spectral group) are not intended for use as fundamental spectral instruments for the orchestra. When they are used they could be put in the proximity of the broad-spectral yangqin, and the bawu or the xiao. The yu and the sheng in modern days are usually all called sheng regardless of the number of reeded pipes. Our distinction here for the purpose of orchestration is to put the harmonic usage on the side of the haidi, the suona, the liuqin and the pipa, and to put the melodic functions (those of the yu) on the side of the di, the guan, the zheng and the konghou.

Regarding the tuning of the string instruments, I propose to respect the natural intervals and the non-equal-tempered performance. The zhongruan should be tuned using an alternating fifth-fourth tuning, and not fifth-fifth. Here the zhongruan is an energetic instrument as we discussed when we analyzed the acoustical and music-psychological role, therefore, we should not treat it strictly as a component of our harmony. This will release the instrument into its more natural role. The compass is not as important as the precision in the natural intervals.

Based in acoustics and based in musical psychology we build the tonal spectra of the Chinese orchestra using the shengguan and the tanbo bases. The music language follows the same threads of thought, to beautify our musical space, to break out of the limits of scale and equal-temperament, and to unlock the new era of orchestral music which inherits the past and inspires the future.

BIBLIOGRAPHY

Shen, Sin-yan, Foundations of the Chinese Orchestra I, *Chinese Music*, **2**, 32 (1979).

Shen, Sin-yan, Foundations of the Chinese Orchestra II, *Chinese Music*, **3**, 16 (1980).

Shen, Sin-yan, What Makes Chinese Music Chinese?, *Chinese Music*, **4**, 23 (1981).

Shen, Sin-yan, Instruments of the Chinese Orchestra, *Chinese Music*, **7**, 33 (1984).

Shen, Sin-yan, The Music of the Chinese Music Society of North America, *Chinese Music*, **9**, 3 (1986).

The Acoustics of Wind Instruments

THE ACOUSTICS OF WIND INSTRUMENTS - A Study in Resonator Design and Performance of Guanyue[5]

The acoustical system used in performance to produce the music of the guanyue, or wind music, is systematically analyzed. The rationale of designs only found in China is explained. Heightened sensitivity to tonal structure produced the unique school of performing arts of wind instruments and the most sophisticated coupled systems used in wind resonators. It led the Chinese to experiment with gradually varying methods of air column excitation and air-column coupling, thus creating the most complete resonators for wind instruments and the most complete techniques for wind performance. The comprehensive system of guanyue: excitation types, resonator types, resonator shapes, and coupled system types are studied. The major acoustical discoveries are discussed.

---

[5] Originally published in two parts in *Chinese Music*, Vol. 13, No. 4 (1990) and Vol. 14, No. 1 (1991).

Chinese Music and Orchestration

INTRODUCTION

Chinese musicians love the full-bodied tone of the large air column and the high frequencies of the short and narrow air column. They also love the contrast between tones of the air column and the most sensitively coupled systems of free reed and air column, and coupled systems of air column and reeded excitation. The oldest group of end-blown flutes known in the world is 8,000 years old. This type of flute was unearthed in the twentieth century (Huang, 1989) and found to contain the complete interval preferences of Chinese music. The end-blown flute utilizes the edge effect -- when a controlled thin stream of air breaks on a sharp edge. Bottle blowers uses this same principle to excite the resonances of the air contained in a bottle. In the end-blown flute, the length of the air column, cylindrical in the dongxiao and slightly conical in the chiba (meaning "a foot and eight inches" in length), is altered by fingering to produce the required fundamental interval relations, and by overblowing. When different lengths of end-blown pipes are used together, the paixiao panpipe is formed. In the last dynasty, the Qing dynasty of China, revivalist activities were prevalent without much musical substance. Ancient instruments were reconstructed by the Qing court according to temperament systems believed to be true and practical without considerations of what musical performance really is and really require. Thus replicas of so-called ancient instruments were produced for the Qing court and for use in ceremonial settings. In particular, the paixiao and the bianzhong, two ancient instruments in the panpipe and in the bell chime family, were reproduced with totally wrong design. The bianzhong replica of the Qing court used bells with round cross-section, which in the face of current research is a joke (see for example Shen, 1987). The paixiao reconstructed used a chromatic arrangement with pitches derived from the method of trisection. The paixiao discovered in the Zenghou Yi

The Acoustics of Wind Instruments

collection (see Lee, 1978) emphasized neighboring minor thirds and major seconds, and further all Zenghou Yi instruments were not tuned to the method of trisection which had been superseded by more superior methods emphasizing physically just intervals.

COUPLED SYSTEMS OF AIR COLUMN AND REEDED EXCITATION

Understanding and utilizing the resonance of an air column, whether cylindrical, conical, or a combination of both, appeared more than 8,000 years ago. The earliest eight-holed vertical flute which was recovered in the twentieth century is 8,000 years old. These vertical flutes principally utilize the edge-effect, which is the bottle-blowing technique many cultures have come to know and love. The development of the practice of musical performance on a single air column by opening successive holes on the body of a flute containing the air column and the practice of musical performance on a series of air columns of successively shorter length apparently developed in parallel. The end-blown bone flute of 8,000 years ago was already so well developed that it contained eight open holes for the performance of all harmonic intervals and two registers. Harmonic intervals are a function of culture. The Chinese culture has a much larger set of preferentially accepted harmonic intervals than the west. It has also invented the resonator systems needed to produce tone qualities and a pitch space now recognized as incredibly complete. The pitch of music is determined by how quickly the vibrating element (reed, air column, string, membrane, etc.) in the instrument and the air which transmits it are vibrating at. For a low note, the air vibrates slowly. For example in playing a C_0, a musician vibrates air at 16 cycles per second. A high note vibrates rapidly. The now

Chinese Music and Orchestration

internationally accepted A_4 vibrates at 440 cycles per second. Registers and intervals are subdivisions of the audible range. Registers divide the audible range into broad areas the size of octaves. Intervals are a more exact measure of pitch-to-pitch distance throughout the range. Pitches are the same distance (interval) apart when the frequency ratio of the notes involved are the same. The globular flute, xun, of 7,000 years ago emphasized a minor third interval. The xun fascinated the west with its intervals (see e.g. Creel, 1937). The paixiao (panpipe) of China and the sheng month organ belong to the other family which utilized bamboo pipes of various lengths, with the paixiao using edge-effect excitation and the sheng family using perfect matches of free reed and air column.

The sheng comes in both open-tube and closed-tube types. In the smaller sheng, each air column in resonance with its free reed is usually open at the top. Each pipe contains a finger hole which when closed sets the pipe in resonance with its free reed, and when open no resonance takes place. The free reed in the bottom of each pipe only partially seals the air blown in when the finger hole is not closed. In larger sheng and the yu, closed pipes are used to conserve air. Each pipe is closed by a key when not fingered. When fingered, the key opens and the air column is set in to resonance with the free reed. The closed pipe system is thus more energy conserving. The principles of acoustical mismatch are widely used in the design of the sheng, the yu, and their accessories (CMSNA, 1980).

The development of Chinese instrumental music benefited from the continuity of the interacting branches of Chinese culture - those of the Yangzi River region, those of the Pearl River region, those of the Yellow River region, those of the Yili River region, and others. Instruments and tonal qualities have come and gone, but the available acoustical systems and accumulated aesthetic appreciation for sound and music persisted. Some have said that Chinese music never developed after a certain point in history, e.g. during or after the Song Dynasty. This is in a sense true

The Acoustics of Wind Instruments

for all of the main resonator types and the preference of intervals appeared to have gone through several complete cycles before.

There are many exceptions of course to this observation which is by no means complete. The development and blossoming of silk and bamboo music is one critical development which defines an important part of Chinese musical art forms today (University of California, 1990).

A MAJOR SCIENTIFIC DISCOVERY: THE TRANSVERSE FLUTE

The transverse flute represents a major breakthrough in the understanding of musical acoustics in the history of mankind. A similar breakthrough is the use of U-tubes in the design of the pipes of wind instruments such as the mouth organs the sheng and the yu. The principle common to all wind instruments is that of an air volume defined by a resonator body. The resonance in the resonator is the source of the sound. This sound becomes music when melodies or harmonies can be produced. In the case of the ancient Chinese instrument the he and the sheng, harmony is primarily produced. In the case of the xiao, the paixiao, the suona, the yu, the oboe, the clarinet, the piccolo, the saxophone, and most other wind instrument including brass instruments, melody is produced. All of the wind instrument listed here are end blown, whether through a reed, a mouthpiece, or through the edge effect directly.

The transverse flute is called hengdi, dizi, or simply di in China. Nowadays the most common flute in the world is the transverse flute. The first transverse flute first appeared in China (Meylan, 1988), and apparently the early Chinese transverse flutes were held to the left. Today most flute players learn to play holding the flute to the right.

Chinese Music and Orchestration

The best known Chinese masters, however, still hold their di to the left (refer to the transverse flute performance of Lu Chun-ling and Wang Tiechui, for example).

The appearance of the transverse flute in China represented a major scientific breakthrough. Utilization of the edge effect in the end-blown vertical flute is natural. Appreciating that the edge effect could be utilized at an edge on a hole on the body of the flute represents the understanding a major acoustical concept - that side-blown excitation can be as effective or more effective than end-blown excitation. Such conceptual developments are plentiful in guanyue development. The earliest side-blown flute was recognized by the flute master Zhao Song-ting (see Qu, 1989) when he studied the bone flutes of Hemudu from 7,000 years ago. In the development of the mouth organs the sheng and the yu, the U-tube was further discovered where small acoustical impedances were used in using air columns which did not have to be straight and were allowed to bend (Shen, 1982).

Two types of transverse flutes were popular in China: the chi which is a closed-tube system, sealed at the right end and usually played with the instrument held to the right, and the di which is an open-tube system described above, often held to the left. Since the discovery of the Zenghou Yi musical treasures of the 5th century BC, the chi has been studied more thoroughly than previously. The chi in the Zenghou Yi version is an interval instrument performing harmonic skeletons emphasizing the preferred interval of minor third. It is held with both hands on the outside of the chi. Two versions of this transverse flute have been observed. The Zenghou Yi version with the five finger holes to the right and the air hole on the left is more common (see Lee, 1979 and Lee, 1980). Another version has the finger hole in the middle of the chi, as described by Needham (Needham, 1962) and as seen in artifacts from the Yangjiawan archeological find of Changsha in Hunan Province. The di has usually six finger holes and is played with crossed

The Acoustics of Wind Instruments

fingering for complex melodies, and is the ancestor of the modern flute and the modi, the di with reed membrane on its body for additional unstable coupling to give the typical Chinese bamboo flute tonal spectrum.

The transverse flute moved through central Asia to Europe, and today all flute players play the transverse flute. The vertical end-blown flute utilizing the edge effect is less known to the west. Vertical end blown flute with a flue is popular in the west and is call the recorder in the west. The flue ensures that the excitation is always controlled and thus instruments with a flue are much easier to play. But the masterly control by good players is what makes end-blown flute without flues what they are musically. They are a whole class above the recorder family in terms of tonal spectrum possibilities and their performance is totally dependent on the skill and the musicianship of the player.

The open-tube transverse flute developed in China through two major acoustical designs: the first with no membrane coupling as in the chi and the hengxiao; the second with active participation of a reed membrane as in the modi, or today's di (dizi).

THE SOUND OF THE SINGLE FREE REED

The paixiao panpipe and the sheng basically differ in the methods of excitation. Both instruments utilize different lengths of air columns. The different-lengthed pipes of the paixiao are excited by the edge effect and therefore depend greatly on embouchure. Each of the sheng pipes is a coupled system of a reed (a free reed unconstrained) and air column. The reed's frequency of vibration matches exactly that corresponding to the height of the air column. Each pipe of the sheng is thus a much more sophisticated music maker than the pipes on the paixiao, thus the

Chinese Music and Orchestration

unique stimulating sound of the sheng pipes in all ranges. In the high range, the high-frequency reed quality dominates, and the sheng is often described as "slightly metallic" in this range. Towards the lower range, the voice of the air column dominates. There the music of the sheng is very much an interestingly modified full-bodied air column.

In the di flute family, the change in pitch is accomplished by changes in the length of air columns configured by fingering a single cylindrical chamber (the flute body). With appropriately placed holes on the flute body, player's fingers control how much of the air in the cylindrical tube is set into vibration. The di further modified the vibration of the air set into vibration by the incorporation of a reed membrane on the body of the tube containing the air column. This membrane therefore must be placed between the air inlet and the first hole, so that all fingering configurations will include the membrane in the path of air vibration.

The single free reed family of instruments is a combination of both types of resonators used in the transverse flute and the sheng. The very popular bawu is a flute (with series of finger holes) supported by a triangular free reed which depresses itself into different positions allowing a large range of quantized free reed frequencies to be generated in resonance with the length of active air column set into vibration by the control of fingering. The single free-reed cannot be overblown effectively, like the case of the single cane reed, such as that on the chalumeau.

The bawu is therefore played without the edge effect. While playing, the player's mouth completely covers the mouthpiece which contains the reed, a triangular tongue cut out of a thin piece of brass, the tongue being the sing free reed capable of many different levels of depression in free vibration coupled to the vibration of the air column. When the bawu is not played, the triangular tongue stays above the brass frame out of which it was cut, the cut being along the equal sides of the isosceles triangle. The base of the triangle is not cut and the base serves as the flexible that bends during the free ringing vibration.

The Acoustics of Wind Instruments

isosceles triangle. The base of the triangle is not cut and the base serves as the flexible that bends during the free ringing vibration.

Few wind instruments have such a variety of tonal coloring as the guanzi, or the saxophone.

HARMONY AND MELODY

From the above discussion, it is obvious that in the development of wind instruments, as in the development of other classes of instruments, melodic and harmonic instruments are used in parallel. In the case of the mouth organ, the yu plays complex melodies, while the sheng harmonizes with harmonic intervals and chords which are harmonic or inharmonic according to the harmonic basis used in the passage. The chi played harmonic intervals and the di played complex melody as flutes. The reason for this complementarity which is always so complete lies in the basic nature of Chinese music which is built on harmony from day one. Melodic progression, temperament theory, and orchestration follow the same harmonic system - as parts of the same cultural acoustics. Thus there was no need in Chinese music to develop scale and harmony separately, as is the case of western music. The notion of the scale does not even exist in Chinese musical literature. But the five complete harmonic skeletons of zhi, shang, yu, jue, and gong dominate music making (Shen, 1981), and temperament choice and orchestration complement each other in real-life applications. The Chinese cultural acoustics is thus driven by harmony, perhaps much more so than any other culture.

The full-bodied guan, or guanzi, with "unflattened" double reed - a totally different concept than double reed.

The Acoustics of Wind Instruments

MUSIC OF THE DOUBLE REED

The most popular group of wind instrument in history is the end-blown flutes. The second most popular group is the double reed. There are two distinct double-reed sub-groups which are acoustically based on the following systems:

(A) The first group uses flattened double reeds. This group include the suona, the haidi, the shawm and the oboe. The player excites the vibration of the air column by first exciting the squeaky sound of the double reed which is flattened. The music that is produced is a result of the sound of the reed, the sound of the air column in close coupling.

(B) The second group uses large and unflattened double reeds. Here the reed is only flattened near the tip. As the player performs, he moves continuously in and out of the unflattened region (see figure of reed on the guanzi). The unflattened part of the reed is critical in producing the most human sound of the shuangguan, guanzi, houguan, and the bass houguan. Here the large reed itself, up to more than three quarters of an inch in width and two to three times that in length is a double reed as well as a strongly resonating air resonator. It couples integrally with the air column of the wooden pipe in performance. The shuangguan has two double-reeded double pipes. The guanzi, the houguan and the bass houguan all utilize a single non-flattened double reed coupled to a cylindrical air column shaped by a highly resonant wooden cylinder. This group of double reed instruments is unfamiliar to musicians of the west. Many western studies merely mention the guanzi as a double reed in the same class as the suona due to lack of familiarity with this type of instrument (see e.g. Joppig, 1988). The reed of the guanzi as discussed above serves two functions. It is both the source of excitation and also a major part of the resonator.

Chinese Music and Orchestration

I once asked a Chinese wind player about the design rationale of the shuangguan which consists of two apparently identical cylindrical guanzi. He replied, "No two reeded tubes have the same tonal spectrum. With two tubes on the shuangguan, the player has control over a broader range of tonal quality and can be more selective of the timber" (Shen, 1987).

Double-piped instruments for this reason of tonal spectrum are very popular in Chinese and other music. Hayashi Kenzo in studies of instruments completely missed this point, and said that "if both pipes produce the same sound, there is no need for two in a group".

This heightened sensitivity to tonal structure led the ancient Chinese to experiment with gradually varying methods of air column excitation and air-column coupling, thus creating the most complete set of resonators and techniques for music of the winds.

THE ENSEMBLE AND ORCHESTRAL ROLES

The general discussion of resonator types and the specific discussions of resonator design for specific performance practices provide the basis for understanding the rich family of guanyue (Chinese wind group). The nomenclature of "shengguan" is used in the orchestral practices, and the Chinese wind group forms a very power fundamental tonal basis for the Chinese orchestra. In the regional orchestras of China, there is usually one first fiddle and one second fiddle. There are sometime a third and a fourth fiddle as well. The Chinese orchestra does not consist of violins or fiddles as fundamental tonal basis (see Note 1 at the end of this paper). The fundamental spectrum of the orchestra or the ensemble is usually one of shengguan (reeded winds) or tanbo (plucked strings). This

The Acoustics of Wind Instruments

was made clear in previous discussions (see p.45-60 and p.117-131). The Chinese Orchestra is thus unique in this sense and the sheng and guan wind instruments must be properly utilized as a group. In this context, the powerfulness of the suona must not be overemphasized (Zhao and Shen, 1988) among the guanyue group.

Chinese traditional orchestration places very high emphasis on tonal differences of the acoustical systems which drive the musical instruments. The xun has in the twentieth century reacquired a role it has not enjoyed for hundreds, if not for thousands, of years. This globular flute of all sizes and design exemplifies the high level of human creativity in vessel blowing and associated understanding of resonator design. The most natural and most human tone of the xun is today appreciated again, now by composers and concert goers as one end of the tonal spectrum, arising from the most complex vibration excited by the simplest edge effect in near-spherical wind chambers. The extent of pitch variation associated with any one fingering is particularly useful in playing ancient and modern classics.

The bili, one of the most popular double reed in the guanzi family, is at the other end of the tonal spectrum. Its large and long reed is coupled to the straight cylindrical tube made of very-high-density wood. This rare coupled system in musical acoustics history has much simpler acoustics compared with the xun, but produced the most powerful and magnetic tone quality that amplified the large and long reed more than the straight air column, producing some of the most unfamiliar sound to modern Western listeners. And yet when modern Western listeners become accustomed to it, it offers the attractive orchestrational component in Chinese orchestral music. In listening and studying "Wailful Wrath by the River" performed on the guanzi by Li Guo-yin, Western trained performers and composers have come to be totally attracted by its tonal magic.

Chinese Music and Orchestration

The harmonizing sheng mouth organ sits in the middle of the tonal spectrum in the Chinese wind ensemble and many Chinese orchestras. This middle ground is awfully wide in spectral compass. Its voice ranges from free-reed dominated pleasant vibration to air-column dominated full-bodied tube sound. It is never at either extreme occupied by the xun or the guanzi. For numerous orchestration styles, it serves a harmonizing purpose that is indispensable. In ensemble music, instruments are always given opportunities to express their individual personality, and yet at other times certain combinations of instruments absolutely require the broad-range middle-ground character of the sheng to provide the ensemble with its characteristic ensemble sound, and the orchestra with its characteristic orchestra sound. The roles of these wind instruments are unfamiliar to modern Western composers. I specially used the term modern Western composers because It is not clear whether in historical times Western musicians had not been in contact with this type of orchestration. In fact judging from the flow of resonator design across the Asian-European continent, it is almost certain that many of the Chinese instruments and their use in ensemble practice, a very old practice, were witnessed by Westerners. But because of the difficulties in long-distance travel, only parts of individual instrument performance and acoustical design were transferred. The broader art and science of ensemble and orchestral practices were lost.

The mid-range suona today popular in Chinese orchestras is an instrument with a special potential. It is a natural double-reed which is not as constrained as the oboe, and yet a good oboe player can probably pick up its techniques in a short time. To play it like a true suona, however, requires complete familiarity with Chinese shengguan music. The mid-range suona, unlike the guanzi at the far end of the shengguan spectrum, has its very mellow range. At the same time at the high and at the low ranges, it is capable of the most interesting improvisational sounds. Jazz musicians who have played it want to find

The Acoustics of Wind Instruments

all the suona in the world. Its acoustical efficiency is also quite a bit higher than the oboe. Its reed is detachable from the mouth piece, so that one can quickly change the style of reed to turn it into a whole new instrument.

Today we reexamine the topic from a practical point of view, of utilizing our understanding in ensemble art and ensemble acoustics. We reviewed the parallel use of melodic and harmonic instruments in the shengguan group. We examines the complete system of acoustical resonators that shape guanyue today. We further looked at the possibilities of the shengguan group as orchestral tonal basis from the standpoint of Shen, 1989 (see p.45-60 of this book). We discover the usefulness of appreciating the philosophical foundation of the shengguan group. This shengguan group is acoustically, technically and tonal spectrum-wise the broadest wind instrument combination anywhere. And the guanyue family, the Chinese winds, offer acoustical, technical, and aesthetic possibilities today to Western musicians and composers not available or not accessible in the past.

Note 1: Overtone characteristics are what separates instruments suitable as fundamental tonal basis for an orchestra to be used in large numbers, from instruments suitable not as orchestrational tonal basis but as single color instruments. In the Chinese orchestral practice through the ages, this has come out loud and clear. Banhu is an outstanding solo instrument, and works well with erhu as its second fiddle, accompanied by plucked strings. Erhu itself is an outstanding solo instrument and works well with wind and plucked accompaniment. But as a group, large numbers of erhu together become a poor component of an orchestra. In recent decades, some composers have imitated the practice of the Western symphony orchestra, and used gaohu and erhu in large groups (e.g. 12 or 24) to establish a bowed string basis. This

Chinese Music and Orchestration

unfortunately works very poorly. Erhu has a drum resonator and is highly individualistic in performance. When it is singing in a background of reeded winds and plucked strings, it carries loud and clear. But when it is used in a larger number, the acoustics is just not there to support a good orchestral tonal spectrum basis. The gaohu fiddle, however, behaves a little better in a group, primarily because it is muted and the python skin is under such high tension that the resonator almost does not behave like a membrane drum but like a very hard drum, making it closer to a wooden drum. Instruments with a wood plate vibration such as the pipa, ruan, qinqin, yangqin which are all plucked in China are much better acoustically to be used as a group. They work together well in large numbers. They are powerful in dynamic range and they are immediately recognized by the music psychology of the audience to serve as a "sound of the orchestra". The erhu group simply does not do that acoustically or music-psychologically when there are other instruments present.

REFERENCES

CMSNA, Exhibition on the Music of the Chinese Orchestra, *Chinese Music*, 3, 60 (1980).

Creel, Herlee Glessner, *The Birth of China*, Ungar, New York (1937).

Hayashi Kenzo, *Dongya Yueqi Kao* (Study of East Asian Instruments, in Chinese), Yinyue Chubanshe, Beijing (1962).

Henan Province Research Institute of Cultural Relics, Henan Wuyang Jiahu Xinshiqi Shidai Yizhi Di Er Zhi Liu Ci Fajue Jianbao (Brief

The Acoustics of Wind Instruments

Report of the Excavation of the Neolithic Sites at Jiahu in Wuyang County of Henan :1st-6th Seasons, in Chinese), *Wenwu*, 1989 Issue Number 1 (1989), 1.

Huang Xiang-peng, Wuyang Jiahu Gudi De Ceyin Yanjiu (Pitch Measurement Studies of Bone Flutes from Jiahu of Wuyang County, in Chinese), *Wenwu*, 1989 Issue Number 1 (1989), 15.

Joppig, Gunther, *The Oboe and the Bassoon*, Amadeus Press, Portland Oregon (1988).

Lee Yuan-Yuan, An Amazing Discovery in Chinese Music, *Chinese Music*, 2, 16 (1979).

Lee Yuan-Yuan, Follow-up on "An Amazing Discovery in Chinese Music", *Chinese Music*, 2, 39 (1979).

Lee Yuan-Yuan, The Music of the Zenghou Zhong, *Chinese Music*, 3, 3 (1980).

Meylan, Raymond, *The Flute*, Amadeus Press, Portland Oregon (1988).

Needham, Joseph, *Science and Civilization in China*, Volume 4: Physics and Physical Technology, Cambridge (1962).

Qu Guang-yi, Woguo Xinshiqi Shidai De Zhuzhi Dilei Yueqi Tuiyi, *Yueqi*, 1989, No. 1, 7 (1989).

Shen, Sin-yan, Acoustics of Ancient Chinese Bells, *Scientific American*, 255, No. 4, 104 (1987).

Chinese Music and Orchestration

Shen, Sin-yan, What Makes Chinese Music Chinese? *Chinese Music*, **4**, 23 (1981).

Shen, Sin-yan, Gamle Kinesiske Klokkers Akustik (in Danish), *Acta Campanologica*, **4**, 141 (1989).

Shen, Sin-yan, Acoustics of Ancient Chinese Bells (in Japanese), *Scientific American* (Tokyo), **17**, 104 (1987).

Shen, Sin-yan, Foundations of the Chinese Orchestra, *Chinese Music*, **2**, 32 (1979).

Shen, Sin-yan, Zhongguo Yinyuejie Dui Renlei Ying Fu De Zeren (in Chinese), *Zhongguo Yinyue*, 1982, No. 2, 18 (1982).

Shen, Sin-yan, The Shanghai Traditional Orchestra and He Wu-qi, *Chinese Music*, **5**, 43 (1982).

Shen, Sin-yan, Foundations of the Chinese Orchestra II, *Chinese Music*, **3**, 16 (1980).

Shen, Sin-yan, On the Acoustical Space of the Chinese Orchestra (in Chinese), *People's Music*, 1989, No. 2, 2 (1989), and p.45-60 of this book.

Shen, Sin-yan, On the System of Chinese Fiddles I, *Chinese Music*, **13**, 24 (1990), and p.117-131 of this book.

Shen, Sin-yan, On the System of Chinese Fiddles II, *Chinese Music*, **13**, 44 (1990), and p.117-131 of this book.

The Acoustics of Wind Instruments

University of California at San Diego Arts & Lectures, Program Notes by Shen Sin-yan for the Silk and Bamboo Ensemble, March 9, 1990 (1990).

Wenhuabu Wenxue Yishu Yanjiushuo Yinyue Wudao Yanjiushi, *Zhongguo Yueqi Jieshao*, Renmin Yinyue Chubanshe, Beijing (1978).

Yue Sheng, *Minzu Yueqi Zhizuo Gaishu*, Qinggongye Chubanshe, Beijing (1980).

Zhao Licheng and Shen Sin-yan, The Music of the Suona, *Chinese Music*, 11, 23 (1988).

ORCHESTRATION WITH CHINESE PERCUSSION INSTRUMENTS[6]

This paper presents a systematic overview of the use of the large number of Chinese percussion instruments. These unique tonal groups are a result of centuries of musical practice, and should only be treated as groups. The individual and orchestrational effects of common groups of Chinese percussion instruments are analyzed, and their musical interest discussed with numerous illustrative examples. This paper is written for both practitioners of the Chinese orchestra and composers for the Western symphony orchestra.

OVERVIEW

Many colleagues have asked me about various aspects of Chinese orchestration, in particular the use of percussion instruments. Many modern Chinese orchestras lack the knowledge of Chinese percussion

---

[6]Originally published in two parts in *Chinese Music*, Vol. 10, No. 3 (1987) and Vol. 11, No. 1 (1988).

Orchestration with Chinese Percussion Instruments

orchestration, and several modern Western composers have expressed their intense interest in integrating Chinese percussion instruments into the symphony orchestra. This paper is written for both groups of audience.

Chinese percussion music is one of the most interesting and highly developed among percussion music in human civilization. The role of the percussion section in all types of Chinese regional orchestras is of paramount musical importance. The role of various Chinese percussion orchestras which feature principally percussion instruments is a unique one in the world, the reason being that these instruments as a group have a myriad of utilization regimes applicable to a multitude of acoustically coherent effects in music making.

Percussion instruments have three basic effects in the Chinese orchestra: rhythmic, decorative, and melodic. Rhythmic effects refer to the most common use in which the ban (clapper), the ling (colliding bells), or the basic combination of gu (drum), bo (cymbals), daluo (large gong) and xiaoluo (small gong) mark the tempo of a passage with a well-defined pattern. Decorative effects refer to the use of characteristic tones of combinations of drums, gongs and cymbals in achieving the desired orchestration objective. Melodic effects refer to the use of definite-pitched percussion instruments including collections of drums, gongs, slit-drums, and xylophones in the performances of single or multiple melodies.

FUNCTIONS AND PERFORMANCE TECHNIQUES

Before I go further into the discussion of orchestration techniques, let us understand the basic functions and performance techniques of the common percussion instruments of the Chinese orchestra.

Chinese Music and Orchestration

Shimianluo, the decorative gong chime of the Chinese orchestra

Orchestration with Chinese Percussion Instruments

Daluo

daluo Large gong of the Chinese orchestra. It is suspended by a string which goes through two small holes on its lip. The string goes through a handle which is held by the left hand. It is performed with a wooden mallet covered by fabric. Three characteristic pitches and tones are produced at the center, near the rim, and in between. It is usually used in conjunction with the xiaoluo, the xiaobo, and the gu. It has loud and bright voices and is used decoratively in the orchestra.

Xiaoluo

Chinese Music and Orchestration

xiaoluo Small gong in the Chinese orchestra, also called the xiluo or neiluo. It has no suspension strings and is pivoted with left hand fingers at its lip. It is played in a vertical position using a thin wooden striker held with the thumb and the middle finger of the right hand in a free-pendulum movement, and produces a bright and crisp sound at the center of the xiaoluo. It has the most dramatic effect among percussion instruments, and together with the daluo, the gu, and the bo forms the basis of the percussion section.

yunluo Chinese fixed-pitched gong chime consisting of a large number of gongs (36, 37 are common) of different thickness but similar surface area suspended on a wooden frame. It is played with a pair of small mallets (hard and soft ones are used). In orchestral performance, the yun-luo is

Orchestration with Chinese Percussion Instruments

used to play melodic passages as well as to outline harmonic skeletons. It has a large dynamic range and a large compass (usually three octaves) and is used as a solo instrument with the Chinese orchestras. A version with ten or more gongs of different surface areas is the shimianluo and is used for tonal decoration in orchestration.

Bo

bo Generic name for a large class of Chinese cymbals consisting of two circular metal plates with hemispherical central sections which allow the bo to attenuate quickly. Silk fabric is tied to a central hole on each hemispherical section for easy holding, and the plates are clashed or a single plate is struck by a mallet during performance. For lingering effects, the nao which has very small central hemispherical sections is used. The bo comes commonly in four sizes: 6 inches, 11 inches, 16 inches, and larger. The bo, the gu, the daluo, and xiaoluo are the four basic components of the percussion section of the Chinese orchestra.

Ling

Chinese Music and Orchestration

ling Colliding bells, also called peng-ling, or xing. It consists of two small hemispherical bells connected by a string and two bells collide at the rim when played. It produces a high-pitched tone pleasing to the ear, and is used rhythmically in the orchestra.

Dagu (or ganggu)

gu Generic name for a large class of Chinese drums. The gu was already popular as a musical instrument in the Shang period (16th Century - 11 Century BC). An ancient gu unearthed in the Yin Ruins of Anyang, Henan Province, has a wooden body and python skin membrane. The common version is called tanggu, or tonggu. It has a wooden frame and both ends of the frame are covered with a skin membrane, usually fabricated from cow hide or synthetic material. The tanggu is suspended by three rings on the frame on a wooden stand and

Orchestration with Chinese Percussion Instruments

is performed with two wooden mallets. There are a number of common versions of the tanggu, the most popular being the large (datanggu) and the small (xiaotanggu). Both are popular in regional orchestras. The small tanggu has a characteristic higher-pitch Chinese tone and is often added to the western symphony orchestra when performing Chinese works. The large tanggu has a range of tones and pitches from the center of the membrane to the frame. It has a very wide dynamic range and is often used to heighten the atmosphere of orchestral compositions. Another common version of large drum for the orchestra is the gang-gu, which is shaped like a flower vase. Its lower membrane is approximately half to three-fifths the size of the top membrane in diameter. It has a mellower tone compared with the large tanggu, and is often used in solo passages. Various sizes of gu are often used in a set in the orchestra. They are not only percussively decorative, but are also melodic.

guban Combination of the high-pitch single-membrane drum, the danpigu, and the clapper, the ban. The combination is performed by a single drum master who controls the percussion section of the Chinese orchestra. The use of the guban drum master gained its prominent position in history during the development of the theatrical orchestras. The pitch requirements of different regions result in a range of sizes of the danpigu, also called bangu. In the Shifangu (ten combination percussion) orchestra of Southern China, the active membrane surface exceeds 1.3 inches. In the Peking Opera orchestra, the active membrane area may be less than an inch. Two strikers known as qian are used in a near-horizontal position for performance. The danpigu is a popular solo instrument in Southern orchestras and acts as a conductor. The "Kuai-gu-duan" (fast drum section) in Shifangu is well-known for the solo danpigu and is virtuosic. The ban clapper, also called tan-ban, consists of two groups of wooden clapper connected with strings. The common version has a single clapper hitting a double clapper and produces a high pitch. The danpigu and the ban, when played together by the drum master of the orchestra, serve as conductor and are jointly called guban. The guban rhythmic patterns are highly varied but are well-known to players of other instruments who listen to the guban for cues to improvisation.

Orchestration with Chinese Percussion Instruments

ORCHESTRATION TECHNIQUES

 Tanggu    Xiaobo

The tanggu and the xiaobo consists of the smallest unit of Chinese percussion instruments. Their effects are rhythmic and decorative. A good example is as follows:

Spring Festival Overture

Li Huanzhi

Chinese Music and Orchestration

Even though other percussion instruments are included, the effect here is mainly due to the small drum tanggu and the high-pitched cymbals xiaobo.

The next percussion unit includes the tanggu, the xiaobo, the daluo, the dabo, and the dagu. A classic example is as follows:

Orchestration with Chinese Percussion Instruments

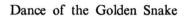

Dance of the Golden Snake

Shen Sin-yan, arr.

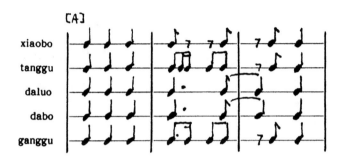

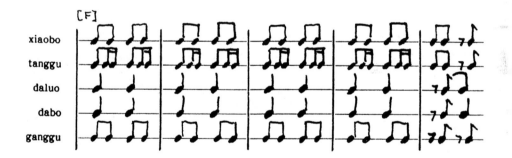

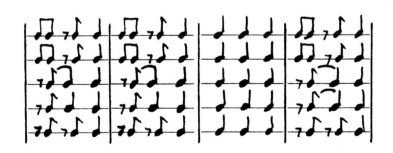

Chinese Music and Orchestration

The daluo and the dabo have long attenuation times, and their rhythmic patterns are suitably decorated by the higher-pitched instruments.

Going from the smallest unit of small drum and cymbal:

    tanggu
    xiaobo

to the larger unit of:

    tanggu
    xiaobo
    daluo (large downward-gliding gong)
    dabo (large cymbal)
    dagu (or ganggu, low drum)

is a major leap in expanding both the gu and the bo systems and in introducing the luo system, the pitch-gliding gongs.

The gong (luo) family is of particular versatility and deserves a detailed discussion.

The large chaoluo is today used extensively in symphony orchestras all over the world. Its center and outer ring are both painted and black and is thus also called black gong. The chaoluo in use come in several sized groups:

(1) 30-45 cm: This sized chaoluo is used in Beijing Opera and in social processionals as a path-clearer.

(2) 50-75 cm: This sized chaoluo is used by medium-sized Chinese and Western Orchestras.

(3) 80-132 cm: This sized chaoluo is used by large symphony orchestras. The largest-sized gong in this category weighs 49 kg.

What is less known internationally is the xiaoluo (the small gongs) of various sizes and musical uses. The xiaoluo produces a "tei" sound.

Orchestration with Chinese Percussion Instruments

After the initially "te" tone, the xiaoluo in a musically interesting way moves up in pitch (the "ei"). This effect is skillfully employed to capture the audience's interest. The orchestral work "Peking Opera Melody" frequently performed by the Orchestra of the Chinese Music Society of North America begins with two tones on the xiaoluo. It is then used throughout the composition in a decorative and rhythmic fashion:

Peking Opera Melody

Gu Guanren

The xiaoluo can be categorized into:

(1) High-pitched xiaoluo: This xiaoluo is pitched between $f_6^{\#}$ and g_6. It is said to have the sound of water and causes excitement in theatrical music.

(2) Medium-pitched xiaoluo: This xiaoluo is pitched between f_6 and $f_6^{\#}$. It has a calm, beautiful voice.

(3) Low-pitched xiaoluo: This xiaoluo is pitched between e_6^{b} and e_6. Its voice is fullbodied and has a strong echo. When used with the low-pitched daluo, it produces a tonal effect preparing the audience for tragedy in the sequence of musical thoughts.

Chinese Music and Orchestration

The xiaoluo should be properly matched with a daluo a fifth below to produce the correct partnership. This is a most versatile instrument that is expected to gain a lot more use and recognition in time to come.

In large-scale composition, the above-discussed units are often combined with theatrical percussion instruments including selected guban systems. The guban (see below) often includes:
- bangu (high-pitch single-membrane drum)
- ban (clapper)

and are different in size and pitch from the South to the North.

The classic "Fishing Song of the East China Sea" employs the following combinations:
- bangu
- tanggu
- fenggu (to simulate effect of the wing)
- xiaobo
- luo chime (consisting of daluo, xiaoluo, chunluo and other decorative gongs arranged according to dominant pitch in the sequence G. A, B, C, D, E, C sharp, G, F)
- small xiaoluo (producing the "dang dang" effect)
- dabo
- daluo
- large daluo.

Here the tanggu, xiaoluo, and dagu supports the wind, the plucked, and the bowed in a rhythmic fashion, and the luo chime often joins in melodic and decorative roles. To produce additional dynamic contrast, the dabo is added.

To produce dramatic effects of combating with the elements, the following percussion combination is used:
- bangu
- fenggu

Orchestration with Chinese Percussion Instruments

       dagu
       luo chime
       dabo
       large daluo
among which the dagu serves as a consistent background providing the tension.

The ling, or colliding bells (see above) can be used alone or with other percussion instruments. The ling bell has both a rhythmic and decorative effect. In "The Moon on High", it accompanies the xiao and the zheng:

In "Spring to a Hundred Households", the ling accompanies the xiao, the zhonghu, and the yangqin:

Chinese Music and Orchestration

Spring to a Hundred Households

Shen Sinyan, arr.

Orchestration with Chinese Percussion Instruments

In "The Peacock Spreads Its Tail", it decorates the orchestral texture:

The Peacock Spreads Its Tail
Tang Kaixuan, arr.

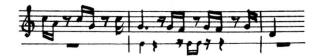

The yunluo gong chime and the shimianluo gong chime is the next group of additions to the above. The shimianluo consists of about ten to fifteen gongs of differing pitch, glides and attenuation. It is usually used as a decorative instrument. Those of us who observed the performance of "Triumphal Song of the Fisherman" by the China Performing Arts Company in the 1970s will no doubt remember its unique orchestrational decoration (see photo on the next page).

The yunluo is a unique solo instrument which has, in a way, replaced the bell chime (bianzhong) and the stone chime (bian qing) of ancient China. Today all three instruments are used together in many orchestras. The yunluo has a repertoire of concerto work. The Qianwei Chinese Orchestra of Jinan, Shandong, for example, has written and performed a significant number of such works.

The yunluo is a powerful harmonic decorator. It takes only a few notes for the harmonic basis set to be outlined:

Chinese Music and Orchestration

Orchestration with Chinese Percussion Instruments

The Unforgettable Water Splashing Festival
Liu Wen-jin

BIBLIOGRAPHY

Shen, Sin-yan, Foundations of the Chinese Orchestra I, *Chinese Music,* 2, 32 (1979).

Shen, Sin-yan, Foundations of the Chinese Orchestra II, *Chinese Music,* 3, 16 (1980).

Shen, Sin-yan, What Makes Chinese Music Chinese?, *Chinese Music,* 4, 23 (1981).

Shen, Sin-yan, Instruments of the Chinese Orchestra, *Chinese Music,* 7, 33 (1984).

Shen, Sin-yan, The Music of the Chinese Music Society of North America, *Chinese Music,* 9, 3 (1986).

Chinese Music and Orchestration

THE TANTIAO (PIPA) STRINGS[7]

This paper is written with the hope that an analysis of the relation between musical instruments in the areas of performing techniques, acoustics and material science will help the reader have a better appreciation of the music produced on the instruments, whether in groups or individually, and in further exploring the potentials of these musical companions created by man.

Among the well-known Chinese plucked strings, the zheng, the se and the yangqin are open-string instruments. On these instruments, the open-string pitches (as opposed to a pitch obtained by stopping the string with a finger) comprise the great majority of pitches taking part in music making (For comparison, consider the piano, the open-string pitches comprise a hundred percent of the pitches taking part in music making). The open-string instruments in general are placed on a table when played, and the plucking movement is perpendicular to the player (towards the player and away from the player). The string-stopping instruments usually are carried in a vertical or a slanted position by the player in music making, with the exception of the qin. The string-stopping plucked strings can be further divided into fretted and fretless

---

[7]Originally published in *Chinese Music*, Vol. 4, No. 1 (1981).

The Tantiao (Pipa) Strings

ones. The popular fretless (finger-board) plucked strings include the qin and the sanxian, and the fretted plucked strings are represented by the ruan, the qinqin, the yueqin, the pipa, the liuqin, and so on.

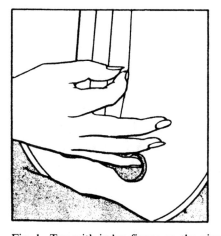

Fig. 1. Tan with index finger on the pipa.

Fig. 2. Tiao with thumb on the pipa.

Chinese Music and Orchestration

The New Plucked Strings - Tantiao System

In terms of performing techniques, the plucked strings can be separated into the "tantiao" category and the "non-tantiao" category. The plucking technique of the sanxian, the ruan, the qinqin, the yueqin, the pipa and the liuqin hinges on the "tantiao" movements. Here "tan" is a leftward (downward) movement, and "tiao" is a rightward (upward) movement (Lee, 1979). In fact, the name "pipa" is synonymous to "tantiao", and has been used since the Qin period (Yang, et al., 1954) to describe the right hand techniques based on a tan and a tiao action. The non-tantiao plucked strings are the zheng, the se, the yangqin and the qin. In a broad sense, the technique of tantiao, or pipa, also encompasses the right hand horizontal plucking movement of fingers such as on the qin, zhen, and se. We shall, however, for the purpose of understanding the detailed physiological involvement in playing plucked strings, restrict "tantiao" to the down-up (or left-right) movement in a plane parallel to the player, as in fingernail- plucking technique of today's pipa, and in plectrum technique of today's liuqin.

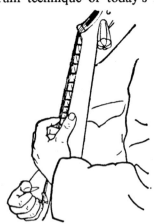

Fig. 3. Tantiao with small plectrum on the liuqin.

The Tantiao (Pipa) Strings

Among the non-tantiao plucked strings, the yangqin is a hammered string instrument, played by striking one or two sets of strings with a bamboo striker held by the player and there are two strikers, one in each hand. The zheng and se both have as many bridges as their strings. The strings are plucked by fingernails of the right and left hand with the left hand fingers also manipulating the tension in the strings for vibrato and ornamentations. The qin is a very impressive instrument. Since it is a string-stopping instrument, a large variety of tonal manipulation is possible. This is why the qin probably has the largest number of notation for tonal expressions among instruments of mankind. Also, since the qin does not have bridges, like in the case of the zheng, the yangqin and the se, the full length of the strings can be set into vibration. The vibration utilizes the full width in space that the instrument occupies.

The earliest tantiao instrument is probably the xiantao. Let us examine this instrument. Early Chinese instruments were divided by the ancients according to the principal material used in the making of the instruments. A member of the skin family (instruments utilizing skin membranes for resonance) was the taogu, or in short, tao. It is a drum with skins on both sides and a holding post. Two bobs are suspended on the frame of the drum so that when the drum is rotated the bobs strike the surfaces of the stretched skin and produce percussive sounds. Such drums are still seen in China in this century, usually carried by itinerant peddlers to attract customers. The taogu is recorded in the Book of Songs, the Book of History, and other well-known documents. There were musicians specializing in the tao during the Zhou period. The tao is also frequently seen in Han murals. The first known tantiao plucked string was developed from the tao. This early plucked string instrument, xiantao, is the ancient sanxian, and appeared no later than the third century BC (the Qin period, Yang, et al., 1954). The meaning of its name is as follows: to stretch string(s) across the surface of the

Chinese Music and Orchestration

drum, and play. This transformation caused the change of a percussive instrument into a new string instrument. Xiantao was performed by the Chinese people when the great wall was being expanded in the Qin period about 214 BC.

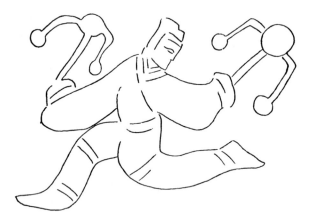

Fig. 4. A mural displaying musician performing the tao.

By the time that the tantiao strings appeared, the Chinese people have loved the musical and acoustical qualities of the string for more than ten centuries, through practices on the qin and other horizontal string instruments. The study of the string has stimulated the development of advanced formulations of harmoniousness in establishing a temperament standard by the division of strings. Using string on the xiantao or the ruan was thus nothing new. Nor was the general utilization of fingers in plucking. On the basis of instrumental development, however, the idea of having the length of the vibrating string exceeding that of the main resonator body was an exciting one, as it made the instruments quite a bit more portable.

The Tantiao (Pipa) Strings

Table 1 Classification of Plucked Strings

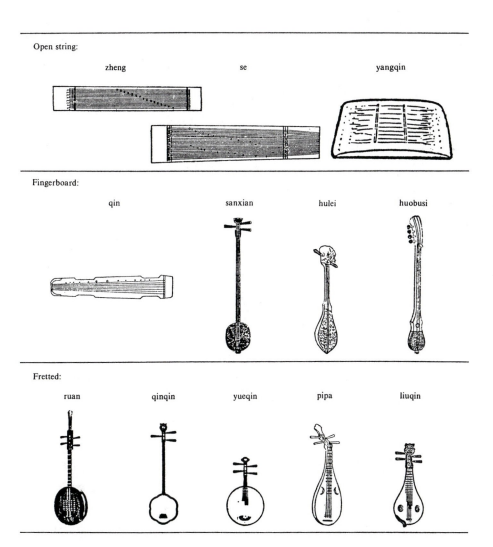

Chinese Music and Orchestration

The development of a tantiao instrument could be along two different lines: (1) to alter the length of the vibrating string by stopping the string onto a fingerboard, and (2) incorporate frets into the instrument and stopping strings onto a fret. The tone produced by the two procedures outlined are quite different. The fretted instrument produces a brighter tone, and can be used to perform small glissando. The fretless finger tone has an intrinsically muffed quality, and the fretless tantiao strings can easily be used to perform large glissando.

The resonator is a key factor in determining the sound produced. Early historic drums of China were made of wood, bamboo, and metal (bronze for example). These practices of material utilization also extended into the making of the drum (resonator) of the tantiao plucked strings. The small drum/long post combination was probably the earliest (as in xiantao). Sanxian, ruan and qinqin belong to this category. Sanxian has a skin-drum as resonator, ruan and qinqin have wooden drums. Sanxian used no frets, and ruan and qinqin have fixed frets.

Fig. 5. The sanxian

The Tantiao (Pipa) Strings

With respect to the choice of string, China is the inventor of silk, which was used to fabricate strings of precision uniformity, at a much earlier time than any other civilization; the number of silk determined the thickness of the string. A large number of early string instruments use silk strings, especially instruments on which the use of harmonics is important. Today, most of the world has turned to metallic strings. But, for reasons of tonal preference, Chinese plucked string players do not settle for completely metallic strings. Metal wound polymer strings are the most popular for the reason of the presence of a fiberlike component in their sound.

According to Cao Anhe, fretted tantiao instruments appeared at about 110 BC (Cao, 1957) in the Western Han period (206 BC-24 AD). Forerunners of the sanxian (fretless), the qinqin (fretted, small resonator), and the ruan (fretted, large resonator) from the Qin and the Han period in general had straight necks and round resonators (Fu, Jin period), and were collectively called "qinhanzi" by later periods.

Fig. 6. The ruan (see Table 2 for acoustical definition).

Chinese Music and Orchestration

The present name "ruan" for the fretted tantiao instruments with a round resonator began in the Tang period. About the time of the Empress Wu (684-704), Jing Lang of Sichuan discovered in an ancient tomb a copper instrument with thirteen frets and a round resonator. He believed it was the instrument that the Jin musician Ruan Xian loved to play, and started calling it ruanxian (Du, Tang period), now abbreviated to ruan. The name is really a symbolic one. Chang Renxia (Chang, 1957) believes that in the Tang period, instrument makers had made ruan out of wood. Thus ruan existed in both copper and wooden forms.

Before Tang, the ruan-type tantiao strings were also called pipa (in addition to the name qinhanzi). The name pipa also means tantiao, as in the principal right hand technique for playing the ruan-type instrument. Lady Zhaojun of the Han period was said to carry a pipa on the horse when she departed to marry the Grand Khan of the Huns. Her pipa was three feet and five inches long and had for strings (Yin, Han period). Looking back today, her instrument must have been a ruan, with a round resonator.

The yueqin which has a short neck, was said to be made by Ruan Xian (Wenxian Tongkao). From the angle of evolution of instruments we might reason that since Ruan Xian was an expert in playing the ruan, he created the yueqin as a high-pitched ruan. Thus, almost all paintings and dramas today are inaccurate in displaying Lady Zhaojun's instrument. They show a pear-shaped resonator (as in today's pipa) instead of a round resonator (as on the ruan, which was called pipa in the Han period).

Du You of the Tang period (Du, Tang period) classified tantiao instruments of his time into (1) qinhanzi, (2) crooked neck pipa, with a resonator large at one end and small at the other end, also called huqin, and (3) five string pipa, smaller than crooked neck pipa. The second and third categories of Du You's classification refer to forerunners of today's pipa. Their resonator has a flat pear-shaped soundboard, a

The Tantiao (Pipa) Strings

convex back, and a crooked neck. Its physical shape is in sharp contrast to that of the ruan, which has a round disc-shaped resonator with flat soundboard and backboard, and a straight neck. Small pipa is seen in murals of tombs in Bangtaizi (Wang, 1979), Liaoning province in northeastern China. The date of the tomb is about late Eastern Han (25-220) or Wei (220-265), possible in the third century. The Dunhuang frescoes contain a large number of pipa, and they date to 4th and 5th century in the Northern Wei period (386-534) AD).

The Influence of the Ruan on the Pipa

When the pear-shaped pipa appeared, it was a relatively primitive instrument in terms of performing techniques, compared to the disc-shaped ruan. It had four frets and was played with a fairly large plectrum. It was mostly held in a near-horizontal position. The ruan then had many more frets (about fourteen), and possessed rather advanced fingernail tantiao techniques, and was played in a near-vertical position to be compatible with its techniques. However, the pipa's very special bodily shape produced sound spectrum of a distinctly different quality from that of the ruan. In order for the pipa to possess at least the range of musical expressiveness and register contrast as the ruan, the natural thing to do was to make performing techniques of the pipa compatible with that of the ruan. In fact, that was what happened. Twelve more frets were added to the pipa, the finger tantiao techniques of the ruan adopted on the pipa, and a near-vertical position for playing the ruan borrowed for the pipa. Today, the old frets of the pipa called "xiang", and the new frets which were added according to ruan practices are called "pin", showing obvious differences in origin.

Chinese Music and Orchestration

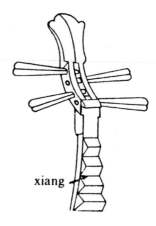

Fig. 7. The older (upper) frets on the pipa known as xiang.

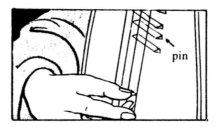

Fig. 8. The newer (lower) frets on the pipa known as pin.

The liuqin and various forms of jingangtui and tupipa are all small pipa. The pipa is typically 100 cm in height and 32 cm in width. The Liuqin is typically 61 cm in height and 22 cm in width. Those small pipa just mentioned have the pear-shaped resonator with a convex back, and pin-frets (no xiang-frets), indicating that they probably are products

The Tantiao (Pipa) Strings

of the marriage of ruan and pipa, for producing a higher-register sound spectrum.

There obviously was a long period of coexistence between various kinds of ruan and various kinds of pipa in music making. The small pipa which is almost the size of a liuqin in the mural of Bangtaizi (3rd century) is shown played in a near vertical (upright) position. Dunhuang frescoes of the 3rd and 4th century have shown the ruan and the pipa in a single mural, both played in the horizontal position. Based on our experience today, fine musical details in various art presentations are not always accurate. Therefore the above observation can only be interpreted

Fig. 9. A crooked-neck ruan.

to mean that the vertical and the horizontal postures of the pipa probably coexisted in the 3rd and the 4th century, with a possible geographical difference in preference of the musicians. The interaction between ruan and pipa also manifests in another interesting example. A Northern Wei mural shows a musician playing a five-string ruan (We call it ruan because it has a disc-type resonator. The shape of the resonator is similar to that of the qinqin.) with a crooked neck as on the pipa. This instrument is shown played with fingers.

Hulei - A Hybrid Tantiao String

Another category of tantiao instrument is worthy of special mention. In the Tang period, a new instrument, hulei, was created. The hulei exists in both large and small sizes, and combines the pear-shaped resonator of the pipa with the python-skin membrane on the sanxian in its resonator. These instrument fortunately still exist today for us to examine. The large hulei is smaller than the pipa. It is about 91 cm in height and 21 cm in width. The small hulei is smaller than the liuqin, about 48 cm in height and 13 cm in width. The range and tone quality of the large hulei is expected to be closest to that of the small sanxian (Shen, 1979).

The huobusi (Yang, 1954, Wang, 1931) is similar to the hulei in that it also combines a wood resonator with a skin membrane. Unfortunately, new huobusi made today (see for example Jia, 1981) is largely simplified. The skin membrane is no longer used, and the new huobusi has nothing but a guitar-like resonator. Material utilization for the purpose of tonal interest seems to be going down hill.

The Tantiao (Pipa) Strings

Table 2 Examples of Acoustical Systems in Tantiao Subgroup of Plucked Strings

System Name	Acoustical Description	Example
Sanxian	resonator (drum) covered with skin membrane on two sides, coupled to a fingerboard neck	large sanxian, small sanxian
Ruan	round disc-like resonator, coupled to fretted neck	ruan, yueqin, qinqin
Pipa	pear-shaped resonator with convex back, with frets	pipa, liuqin

Conclusion

We have in this paper centered on a number of popular members of the plucked strings, which in total would account for about half of all Chinese strings. The bowed strings which are not discussed here are also intimately related to the plucked strings studied here. The bowed strings have been dealt with individually in detail in previous papers (Shen, 1979, Shen, 1979, Lee, 1979, Liu, Shen 1977), and they will be treated collectively in a forthcoming paper (Shen).

Chinese Music and Orchestration

It is evident that the Chinese-plucked strings have been built up systematically over the centuries of practical utilization to reach a remarkable state of musical capabilities. Many examples of string instrumentation (Exhibition, 1980) indicate that the Chinese people love the tonal color and the melodic quality of the plucked-string component of the Chinese orchestra. Xiansuo Shisan Tao (Ng, 19870) which consists of thirteen pieces for the strings, in the version that Rong Zhai left us, uses the sanxian, the pipa, the zheng, the huqin, and a number of other instruments (the xiao, the di, the sheng, the tiqin, the guan, the jiu yunluo, the xiao tanggu or the peng zhong). The four principal lead instruments thus consist of three plucked and one bowed members. The Henan Bantouqu (Shen, 1979) orchestration utilizes the zhuihu, the erhu, the jinghu, the sheng, the di, the pipa, the sanxian, the zheng, the danpigu, and the ban, but the lead instruments are the zhuihu, the pipa, the sanxian, and the zheng. Once again the orchestration favors three plucked and one bowed members. Unfortunately, a number of composers have shown no understanding of these orchestration practices which are loved by the large majority of the Chinese. They turned to an erhu-based orchestra, in light of the bowed-string-based orchestration of the Western symphony orchestra, without much success.

REFERENCES

Lee, Yuan-yuan, The Liuyeqin and Wang Hui-ran, *Chinese Music*, 2/2, 6 (1979).

Referential Photographic Documentation on Chinese Music History, edited by Yang Yin-liu, et al., New Music Publisher, Shanghai (1954).

The Tantiao (Pipa) Strings

Cao, Anhe, Introduction to Pipa, in *A Collection of Papers on the Study of National Music*, the Music Publisher (1957).

Fu, Xuan, *Pipa Fu* (Jin period).

Du, You, *Tongdian*, (Tang period).

Chang, Ren-xia, in *A Collection of Papers on the Study of National Music*, the Music Publisher (1957).

Yin, Shao, *Fengsu Tong*, (Han period).

Wenxian Tongkao.

Wang Zeng-xin, Liaoyangshi Bangtaizi Erhao Bihua Mu, *Kaogu*, 1960/1.

Shen, Sin-yan, Foundation of the Chinese Orchestra (1), *Chinese Music*, 2/3, 32 (1979).

Shen, Sin-yan, Foundation of the Chinese Orchestra (2), *Chinese Music*, 3/1, 16 (1980).

Wang, Guangqi, *A History of Chinese Music*, Taiping Book Co., (1962 printing, book written in 1931).

Jia, Weihan, The Origin and Reformation of the Mongolian Plucked String Instrument - Huobusi, *Yueqi* 1981/1.

Shen, Sin-yan, Erhu, *Chinese Music*, 2/1, 2 (1979).

Chinese Music and Orchestration

Shen, Sin-yan, The Music of Liu Ming-yuan, *Chinese Music*, 2/2, 3 (1979).

Lee, Yuan-yuan, Fantasy on the Sanmen Gorge, *Chinese Music*, 2/2, 23 (1979).

Liu, Ming-yuan, Banhu, *Chinese Music*, 4/2, 28 (1981).

Shen, Sin-yan, The Application of Bowed Strings in Chinese Music, *Music and Audiophile*, No. 46 (March 20, 1977).

Exhibition on the Music of the Chinese Orchestra, University of Chicago, USA, August 11-12, 1980.

Ng, Kok Koon, Xiansuo Shisan Tao - A Study (I), *Chinese Music*, 3/2, 42 (1980).

The System of Chinese Fiddles

On the System of Chinese Fiddles[8]

The complete system of Chinese fiddles is discussed in terms of performance art, acoustics, and orchestral roles. The successful artistry of the Chinese fiddles generically known as huqin is attributed to the creative use of acoustics of the instrument in performance techniques, the tradition of fixed position glissando, tension-altering vibrato called kouxian, and the art of temperament use. Examples from recordings of Liu Ming-yuan, Wang Guo-tong, and Liu Tian-Yi illustrate the analysis.

General Discussion

The fiddles of China are mostly <u>true bowed strings</u>, meaning they were originally designed for use as a bowed string instrument, rather than reconstructed from a plucked string instrument as is the case of the

---

[8]Originally published in two parts in *Chinese Music*, Vol. 13, No. 2 (1990) and Vol. 13, No. 3 (1990).

Chinese Music and Orchestration

violin. This fact is also reflected in their performing techniques. The Chinese fiddles are predominantly bowed when they are played, and the performing techniques of the right hand bowing and left hand fingering reached great heights. The tension on all Chinese bows are controlled by the player while playing. On the violin, once the tension in the bow hair is fixed, it is fixed for the entire movement or the entire piece, except for some transient changes in the tension when the bow hair is pressed hard against a string. The left hand techniques for the Chinese fiddles are probably the most highly developed and the most systematic in the world. Many of these techniques utilize fully the acoustics of these instruments (both with membrane resonator and box resonator). The violin today still show clearly its connection with its plucked ancestors. The desire to do double stopping and the desire to play three to four strings at a time resemble the desire to strum, and are obvious proofs of the above-mentioned linkage with its plucked ancestors of the pipa (principal Chinese plucked strings) family.

In this paper I will discuss the system of Chinese fiddles with the objective of providing the readers as much intuitive understanding of the instruments, their role in ensemble and orchestra playing, their use of acoustics , their performing artistry, and artists. When ever possible, existing recording are used to illustrate my points.

Erhu - The Most Popular Second Fiddle

The most popular fiddle of China today is certainly the erhu (for an overview of the erhu, see Shen, 1979). It is an instrument that is the dream of every fiddle student, even students of plucked strings. A major reason for the erhu's popularity is due to its orchestrational role in regional orchestra. It is the most important second fiddle in almost all

The System of Chinese Fiddles

regional orchestras, second only to such first fiddles orchestrationally as banhu, jinghu, gaohu (yuehu), zhuihu, touxian and others (for the large variety of material that is used to make these instruments, refer to Yue Sheng, 1980). Here banhu is the first fiddle in the music of Qinqiang (Shaanxi Province) and other bangzi (clapper opera, popular in Shanxi Province, Hebei Province, Inner Mongolia, and other Northern Chinese Provinces) music. Jinghu is the first fiddle of Jingju (Peking Opera). Gaohu, or also known as yuehu is a first fiddle of the Cantonese orchestra (Guangdong Province, now popular nationwide) with erxian being the other first fiddle. Zhuihu is the first fiddle of Luju (Shandong Province) in which it is also called zhuizi or zhuiqin. The zhuihu is also the principal instrument of Henan Zhuizi, ballad singing popular in Henan, Anhui and Shandong Provinces. Touxian is the first fiddle of Chaozhou music from the Shantou area and vicinity in Guangdong Province where the Chaozhou dialect (Teochew) is spoken. Of course there are many types of regional orchestras in which the erhu is not used or hardly used. But because of the wide geographical coverage of the types of orchestras in which the erhu is used, and its artistic potential, the erhu became the most important Chinese fiddle, even overseas.

The acoustics of the most of the erhu made today (they correspond to the zhuyin erhu of the first half of the twentieth century, where "zhuyin" is an orchestrational term referring to the first part of an erhu duet, and the second part is played on a tuoyin erhu) which is a drum fiddle with python skin as the membrane is such that the most appropriate tuning to obtain a full resonance is have middle C as the lowest pitch. Another popular version called the tuoyin erhu has a larger resonator and uses thicker strings has acoustics such that the fullest resonance is achieved when the lowest pitch is tuned a fourth lower than the erhu (the zhuyin erhu) at G. The zhonghu is a version similar to the tuoyin erhu. During the time of Liu Tian-hua in the 1930s he standardized the erhu (zhuyin erhu) to a tuning having a lowest

Chinese Music and Orchestration

pitch of D. The erhu however is capable of being tuned both C and D as the lowest pitch, with C usually better in resonance. The instrument makers of the Beijing National Instruments Factory have in recent years also perfect a design of the erhu very suitable to the higher tuning (D lowest). The "changcheng erhu" used today in performing "The Great Wall" by Liu Wen-jin is really like the original zhuyin erhu.

The Artistry of the Chinese Fiddles

Chinese music is a rare breed of music that has existed continuously for over 8,000 years. The earliest instrumental ensemble music as an art form first appeared in the Chinese civilization. It is a branch of human civilization that has contributed to and interacted with civilizations of all major continents throughout history. The appearance of the concept of instrumental music as an art form to be appreciated independent of vocal music drove Chinese music to new heights in early music history. The long tradition of well-established aesthetic values and manners of musical interpretation made Chinese music one of the hardest to learn in the world. The broad all-encompassing appreciative capacity of Chinese musicians also made the Chinese people one of the easiest to adapt to performance of music of many other cultures. At this time in history when Chinese culture is at a difficult crossroad (see e.g. discussions in Li, 1982, and Shen 1982 for the situation then. It is truly at a crossroad now) I find it even more important to write this paper to examine Chinese fiddle music as a system because it is the only way the fiddle music of China can be properly and easily understood as a whole. The discussion will thus be one of music and will go beyond anthropology or ethnomusicology.

The System of Chinese Fiddles

The existing recording of fiddle music by such masters as Liu Mingyuan (banhu), Wang Guo-tong (erhu), and Liu Tian-Yi (gaohu) is a good starting point for an overview of Chinese fiddle artistry. The musical interest of these masters can be classified into the following sources:

(A) Creative use of the acoustics of the instrument. The banhu, for example, is a wood fiddle whose plate vibration is extremely strong when open strings are played. The contrast of these open-string tones and other tones, in particular, the minor third above each open string provides a very attractive effect. The musical psychology of this effect is as follows. When an open-string resonance is followed by a small glide upward to a minor third above, that minor third is enhanced by a tension which is provided by the reverberation of the open string. When a tone beginning with first finger on the minor third above an open string is followed by a long glide to open string, the open string comes as a shock, and a pleasant shock to the audience because of its energy content. A similar, but not as strong, effect is available between the an open string resonance and the perfect fourth above it. Frequently, a mere glide suggesting it might approach an open string produces the same musical psychology. Liu Ming-yuan in "Year of Happiness" (Xing Fu Nian, refer to M-456 and M-458 recorded by the China Record Company) utilized precisely these effects in interpreting repeated notes. In "The Music of Liu Ming-Yuan" (Shen, 1979) I wrote "he performed with such joy and virtuosity that those leading passages on the banhu in "Year of Happiness" remain today one of the most treasured recordings of banhu music...Liu Ming-yuan is probably the most gifted banhu player in this century". The musical interests in another piece for the zhonghu "On the Prairie" (Caoyuan Shang, refer to M-597 and S-0027 recorded by the China Record Company) also come from maneuvering open-string resonance and harmonics. These effects are not possible to produce on the violin, and banhu artists like Liu Ming-yuan truly contribute to the

Chinese Music and Orchestration

fun of listening to fiddle music. The comparison with the violin is made here because both the banhu and the violin are box-type fiddles based on plate vibration.

(B) Fixed position glissando. In my own performance of the erhu, I have found fixed position glissando (dingba huayin) and padded glissando (dianzhi huayin) to be most attractive forms of expression and embellishment for my audience. Chinese music, as I have said so many times, cannot be treated strictly on the basis of scales. For example, in "The Moon Mirrored in Erquan" (Erquan Yingyue), there are numerous places where a "mi" approaches a "sol" a minor third higher via an infinite number of intervals narrower than a minor third. In many transcription, those intervals were either written as a half tone or a full step. But musically, depending on the mood of performance, any of the above infinite number of choices could be right, except the half tone and the full step. This thus presents a problem for many players who interpret from transcribed scores. When those scale-step (including chromatic) based intervals were used, the musical interest goes to zero, because only the minor third formed by the ends of "mi" and "sol" are meant to be exact, and the intermediate intervals were ways of musically suggesting that exact interval as an objective. This is a rather difficult concept to accept at first if you are trained in institutionalized Western music which treats scales as sacred. But in Chinese music, especially fiddle music, the artistry involves very different concepts of music, some of which had been lost in the institutionalization of music today. Fixed position glissando lends itself effectively to such infinite choice of intervals in embellishing another exact interval that is just. The concept of the musical interest associated with fixed position glissando was brought out in my analysis of the works of A Bing and his performance. Both "Erquan" and "Listen to the Pine" (Ting Song) are excellent examples for such expressions. "The Great Wall" (Chang Cheng) has fixed position

The System of Chinese Fiddles

glissando passages, but many other recent compositions simply do not show the very special qualities of the erhu.

(C) The art of temperament use. Chinese music never accepted the equal temperament system even though it was first invented in China. The rejection did not come as a result of sudden decision, but was a result of infinite numbers of real-life experimentation with music performance. Today we are witnessing new music in the Western world move away from equal tempered intervals in search of new musical interest. The same concepts had been tested in the course of Chinese music history. The Chinese musician in all of the temperament oscillation cycles in the centuries always returned to recognition of the just intervals. In so doing, the Chinese musician has also arrived a highly developed system of using sub-divisions of just intervals, which are to be contrasted with just intervals. They have also recognized and used a much wide range of intervals from the harmonic series. Gaohu artist Liu Tian-Yi and banhu artist Liu Ming-yuan are two of the artists whose performances and recordings have reached heights in the use of temperaments. Yehudi Menuhin recorded Liu Tian-Yi in his television series on music appreciation, in which the gaohu performance was at the highest level possible and the temperament art in "Birds Return to the Woods" (Niao Tou Lin) was at its best. "Birds Return to the Woods" (Niao Tou Lin) can be heard on M-086 issued by the China Record Company. Wang Guo-tong's early recordings of erhu music including "Fantasy on the Sanmen Gorge" (Sanmen Xia Changxiangqu) also reflected the artistic choice of temperaments, but some of his more recent recordings have tended to move in the equal-tempered direction, thus reducing the musical interest of the erhu music. Lee Yuan-Yuan calls "Fantasy on the Sanmen Gorge" the most brilliant composition for the erhu (Lee, 1979). The recordings DM-6127 recorded by Wang Guo-tong and issued by the China Record Company and CMS101 and CMS102 recorded by Shen

Chinese Music and Orchestration

Sin-yan and issued by the Chinese Music Society of North America are some of the examples demonstrating the powerful technique of kouxian which rapidly alters the string tension in contrast with rolling vibrato. The purposely sharpened temperament makes erhu music what it is. Yu Qi-wei on the gaohu is another artist whose performance and recordings can be outstanding in this respect of perfecting temperament art. You probably wonder why don't I treat these performances as on a different tuning system. The reason is that I do not think it would be fair to the Chinese musicians who have elevated temperament use in fiddle performance to an art.

In the program notes for "The Moon Mirrored in Erquan" (see e.g. Program Notes, Silk and Bamboo Ensemble of the Chinese Music Society of North America, University of California at San Diego, Price Center, March 9, 1990), I wrote "A number of the most important methods of expression on the erhu is to be noted: 1. open-string grace note to decorate the note a whole step above, 2. sudden pause of the bow following a long bow ending on a minor third above the main note, 3. fixed position glissando, and 4. bowing to alter the relative weight of strong and weak beats". The first and second are examples of some of the finest style of embellishment in erhu performance. The same type of expressions can also be found clearly in the performance of "Joy of Xiangjiang" (Xiangjiang Le) performed by Li Bing-yuan. The third is fixed position glissando, and the fourth refers a comparison with Western music. Chinese music should never be artificially cast into measures in the first place. Even if some simple rhythm (e.g. 2/4) is apparently present, the relative strong and weak beats are "wrong" by Western standards. This is the source of a lot of confusion in Chinese violin music. The Chinese violin schools have worked hard to assimilate the art of the erhu, but without much success. The reason is a simple one. The artistic frame of mind of many of these violin music composers and

The System of Chinese Fiddles

performers is a Western one. The cultural context is wrong and the artistic expression suffers.

The cultural context we are talking about here is a very real and quantifiable one. The descriptions I have used above are just some of the ways a step-by-step understanding of the exact nature of the source of musical interest can be achieved. Without such quantitative description, discussions do not do much good.

Ensemble Roles of the Chinese Fiddles

In the regional orchestras of China, there is usually one first fiddle and one second fiddle. There are sometime a third and a fourth fiddle as well. The fundamental spectrum of the orchestra or the ensemble is usually one of shengguan (reeded winds) or tanbo (plucked strings).

The reason is one of acoustics (see e.g. Shen, 1989). In the 1970s I discussed this problem with Arthur Benade. We came up with a theory that overtone characteristics are what separates instruments suitable as fundamental tonal basis for an orchestra to be used in large numbers, from instruments suitable not as orchestrational tonal basis but as single color instruments. In the Chinese orchestral practice through the ages, this has come out loud and clear. Banhu is an outstanding solo instrument, and works well with erhu as its second fiddle, accompanied by plucked strings. Erhu itself is an outstanding solo instrument and works well with wind and plucked accompaniment. But as a group, large numbers of erhu together become a poor component of an orchestra.

In recent decades, some composers have imitated the practice of the Western symphony orchestra, and used gaohu and erhu in large groups (e.g. 12 or 24) to establish a bowed string basis. This unfortunately

Chinese Music and Orchestration

works very poorly. Erhu has a drum resonator and is highly individualistic in performance. When it is singing in a background of reeded winds and plucked strings, it carries loud and clear. But when it is used in a larger number, the acoustics is just not there to support a good orchestral tonal spectrum basis. The gaohu, however, behaves a little better in a group, primarily because it is muted and the python skin is under such high tension that the resonator almost does not behave like a membrane drum but like a very hard drum, making it closer to a wooden drum. Instruments with a wood plate vibration such as the pipa, ruan, qinqin, yangqin which are all plucked in China are much better acoustically to be used as a group. They work together well in large numbers. They are powerful in dynamic range and they are immediately recognized by the music psychology of the audience to serve as a "sound of the orchestra". The erhu group simply does not do that acoustically or music-psychologically when there are other instruments present.

Some of the winning combinations are:

One jinghu, supported by one erhu, supported by a group of plucked strings.

One banhu, supported by one to three erhu, supported by a group of reeded winds and a group of plucked strings.

Solo erhu, supported by full orchestra of reeded winds and plucked strings, and percussions.

Solo erhu, supported by Western symphony orchestra.

The System of Chinese Fiddles

One zhuihu, supported by one to two erhu, supported by full orchestra of reeded winds and plucked strings, and percussions.

One gaohu, supported by one zhonghu, supported by plucked strings and reeded winds.

The systematics is based solidly on acoustics and performance style, and has been tested over a long period of time.

Special Notes on the Chinese Fiddle Classification

The Chinese fiddles can be classified into those with no finger board and those with finger board. The performance art of the two categories in the Chinese fiddle system are distinctly different.

Most listeners of Chinese music are more familiar with the fiddles with no finger board which are thus capable of both rolling vibrato and tension-altering vibrato. These include the erhu, jinghu, banhu, sihu, matouqin, ruangong huqin and many others. As discussed above in the context of the banhu, many of these classical fiddles are characterized acoustically by their exceedingly strong open-string resonance which is present when used properly in many overtones. The tradition of compositions has fully utilized this character. The finger board varieties are not capable of much tension-altering vibrato, and are thus very different in performance style. The open-string resonance is also much less important in compositions for the finger board fiddles, except for the use of the open strings themselves to define the harmonic basis, a

Chinese Music and Orchestration

practice not limited to the fiddles but to all Chinese instruments. They favor very large glides, up to octave intervals and beyond.

Three of the favorite finger board Chinese fiddles are the zhuihu, the leiqin, and the aigan zhuihu (short-post zhuihu). Zhuihu performance is shown below.

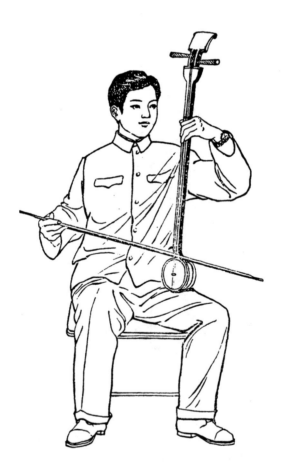

The System of Chinese Fiddles

The zhuihu is the first fiddle of the Luju Opera (for the use of the zhuihu or zhuiqin in Luju Opera see Gao, 1983) of Shandong Province. Its other names include the zhuiqin and the zhuizi (after which the Henan ballad singing known as Henan Zhuizi is named). A common zhuihu is a membrane instrument with a cylindrical resonator covered with python skin, and has a very long finger board. The tuning for the strings is a perfect fourth apart. Some zhuihu uses a sanxian-like resonator but uses wood plate vibration on a near-square resonator (This version is usually called zhuizi, see e.g. Wenhuabu Wenxue Yishu Yanjiushuo Yinyue Wudao Yanjiushi, 1978). The compass is usually a-d^3. The E and A strings of the pipa can be used on the zhuizi (zhuihu). The instrument is placed on the left lap and is placed with the fingerboard absolutely vertical, to permit natural and accurate glides. Classical and folk performers classify the zhuizi and the zhuihu into many different instruments and also into many styles of performance. But since the basic performance art is of the same type we have grouped them together here as zhuihu.

Leiqin was modified from zhuiqin by Wang Dian-yu. A copper cylinder was introduced for the resonator with a python skin membrane. The leiqin is capable of large dynamic contrast and is typically tuned a fifth apart. The art of the leiqin has evolved into an instrumental class all by itself, with a lot of its repertoire strictly for instrumental performance. But the source of the music is still very much connected with theatrical music and ballad singing (see e.g. Zhao, 1982).

The aigan zhuihu (short-post zhuihu) is used with the sihu and the erhu in the Erjiaxian orchestra (for a history see Ni, 1983), popular in Southwestern Shandong, Eastern Henan, Northern Henan, Northern Anhui and vicinity. The name Erjiaxian comes from the fact that the lead instrument in it the sihu has two bunches of horse hairs thus "er" for two, "jia" for sandwiched, and "xian" for strings. The aigan zhuihu is a higher pitched zhuihu with a short post. It is today used as a lead

Chinese Music and Orchestration

solo instrument supported by plucked strings, reeded winds and percussion.

References

CMSNA, Exhibition on the Music of the Chinese Orchestra, *Chinese Music*, **3**, 60 (1980).

Gao, Fu-liang, *Zhuiqin Yanzou Jichu* (in Chinese), Shandong Renmin Chubanshe, Jinan (1983).

Lee, Yuan-Yuan, Fantasy on the Sanmen Gorge, *Chinese Music*, **2**, 23 (1979).

Li, Jian, Kai Chang Bai (in Chinese), *Lianhe Yinyue*, February, 1982, United Music Academy, Hong Kong (1982).

Ni, Shu-ren, *Erjiaxian Changqiang Yinyue Chutan* (in Chinese), Shandong Renmin Chubanshe, Jinan (1983).

Shen, Sin-yan, Erhu, *Chinese Music*, **2**, No. 1 (published as *Chinese Music General Newsletter*, Vol.79, No. 1), P.2 (1979).

Shen, Sin-yan, Foundations of the Chinese Orchestra, *Chinese Music*, **2**, 32 (1979).

Shen, Sin-yan, What Makes Chinese Music Chinese? *Chinese Music*, **4**, 23 (1981).

The System of Chinese Fiddles

Shen, Sin-yan, Foundations of the Chinese Orchestra II, *Chinese Music*, 3, 16 (1980).

Shen, Sin-yan, Zhongguo Yinyuejie Dui Renlei Yingfu De Zeren (in Chinese), *Lianhe Yinyue*, February, 1982, United Music Academy, Hong Kong (1982).

Shen, Sin-yan, On the Acoustical Space of the Chinese Orchestra (in Chinese), *People's Music*, 1989, No. 2, 2 (1989).

Shen, Sin-yan, The Shanghai Traditional Orchestra and He Wu-qi, *Chinese Music*, 5, 43 (1982).

University of California at San Diego Arts & Lectures, Program Notes by Shen Sin-yan for the Silk and Bamboo Ensemble of the Chinese Music Society of North America, March 9, 1990 (1990).

Wenhuabu Wenxue Yishu Yanjiushuo Yinyue Wudao Yanjiushi, *Zhongguo Yueqi Jieshao*, Renmin Yinyue Chubanshe, Beijing (1978).

Yue Sheng, *Minzu Yueqi Zhizuo Gaishu*, Qinggongye Chubanshe, Beijing (1980).

Zhao, Yuzhai, My Career as a Musician, *Chinese Music*, 5, 63 (1982).

Chinese Music and Orchestration

THE SHANGHAI TRADITIONAL ORCHESTRA AND HE WU-QI[9]

During 1950s and 1960s, some of the best recordings of traditional Chinese instrumental music were available. The recordings included a fairly large number of top-level musicians from all of the provinces. Among the orchestra and ensemble music recorded, those from the Shanghai Traditional Orchestra no doubt stand out both in quality and quantity. This paper discusses the musical achievements of the Shanghai Traditional Orchestra as witnessed on these recordings.

INTRODUCTION

Those of us who kept good track of the publications of recordings of Chinese music saw the emergence of a group of outstanding performing artists of Chinese musical instruments in the 1950s from Shanghai. These

---

[9] Originally published in *Chinese Music*, Vol. 5, No. 3 (1982).

Shanghai Traditional Orchestra

musicians were associated with the Shanghai Traditional Orchestra of Shanghai. The best Shanghai-styled orchestral music recorded to-date including "Wedding Processional", "Zhonghua Liuban", "Sanliu", "The Song of Joy" were performed by the Shanghai Traditional Orchestra. As Chinese records often do not contain complete program notes, most of the time we were unable to track down on the performers and the composers/arrangers whose work was recorded. As different versions of the recordings were published over the years, we gradually were able to recognize some of the names which appeared most frequently and it also became increasingly easier to associate the artistic style of a recording with the musicians, including both performers and composers. Several important names have been associated with the Shanghai Traditional Orchestra for the past thirty years. In particular, music director He Wu-qi, composers Gu Guanren, Zeng Jia-qing, Ma Shenglong, and virtuoso artists Lu Chun-ling, Xiang Zu-hua, Pan Miao-xing, and others have inspired many an audience from continent to continent, through their recordings.

HE WU-QI - A DYNAMIC DIRECTOR

He Wu-qi was probably the most important music director of China in this century. In a time of steady decline in societal interest towards Chinese classical music, He Wu-qi revitalized the musical scene. He must have inspired his orchestral members of the Shanghai Traditional Orchestra so much that music created by this group during those years of the 1950s and the 1960s were full of such unlimited energy, delicate and full-bodied expressions, and extra-ordinary musical perception.

Chinese Music and Orchestration

The performance of the Shanghai Traditional Orchestra under He Wu-qi showed extreme coherence in orchestral interpretation of music, and command of instrumental practices which was built upon the understanding of sources of musical interest developed along a continuous history of more than eight thousand years of field practices. The performance of "The Ma An Shan Overture", composed by He Wu-qi, and directed by He Wu-qi, "Galloping on the Prairie", composed by Lu Chun-ling and Gu Guanren, and directed by He Wu-qi, "Fishing Song of the East China Sea", composed by Ma Shenglong and Gu Guanren, and directed by He Wu-qi, were some of the best examples in this category. Let us examine below some of the musical factors which contributed to the success of these performances.

"The Ma An Shan Overture" combines in an unusual manner elements of musical interest of both the north and the south. As we know, the province of Jiangsu, in which Shanghai is a major region, borders the provinces of Anhui, and Shandong. The orchestral music of Anhui often shows a broad, free and easy kind of gracefulness with no trace of constraint. The music of Jiangsu is characterized by its smoothness in musical flow and implicitness in expression, and Jiangsu's silk and bamboo orchestration is unmatched in beauty and charm. He Wu-qi in "The Ma An Shan Overture" captured both the Shanghai-styled beauty and the broadness of the music of Anhui and the North. He used the sonorous banhu to lead a silk and bamboo textured continuum, with remarkable support on the large sanxian and the plucked strings, and Shanghai-styled erhu in unison as a special element tonal design. In addition to using the above combinations of instrumental groups, a lovely short middle passage with the sheng (mouth organ) taking the lead was most satisfying to the ear.

In the very first section, the banhu leading a silk and bamboo spectrum, with the banhu performing prominent glissandos on immediately repeated notes (see*):

Shanghai Traditional Orchestra

In the passage that follows, the texture of the orchestra changes completely. First the di is supported by the plucked strings, and then the same passage is repeated with the warm sound of the erhu group:

In the next transitional passage, the banhu, the sizhu (silk and bamboo) and the percussion group counterbalance to create an unstable block of measures:

leading to a complete return to the tonic (D). Section two then begins in the most cheerful and carefree atmosphere with the shen accompanied by the plucked strings:

This is reiterated using the heart-warming erhu group in place of the sheng.

Chinese Music and Orchestration

Before the music returns to the original texture with the banhu leading the silk and bamboo, it goes through another transitional passage in which the sudden emergence of a full but transparent chord on the sheng produces unbelievable tonal interest:

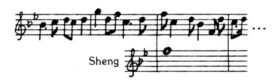

The rhythmic patterns of some of the passages are worthy of special mention. In performing "The Ma An Shan Overture", everybody remembers the series of Northern-styled separated bowing which goes through such intricate melodic progression that makes it full of fun.

In section two, the main solo melody is supported by the broadest, the most confident-sounding background of register-contrasting plucked rhythm:

Shanghai Traditional Orchestra

The musical expressions of "The Ma An Shan Overture" demands the most precise control of a wide contrasting dynamic range. Very simple percussion instruments are used (the bo takes the lead), but they blend extremely well with the instrumental groups outlined above.

The melodic design was compact, uninterrupted, and leads you all the way to the end without an opportunity to pause even momentarily, In my opinion, "The Ma An Shan Overture" has one shortcoming; It is too short.

"Galloping on the Prairie" is one of the best orchestrated composition in the last thirty to forty years. It is a piece written for the di (reeded bamboo flute) and the traditional orchestra. The Shanghai Traditional Orchestra's recording of this music under the direction of He Wu-qi will probably never be surpassed in artistic achievements. The performance fully exploited the unexpected effects of the combination of the voice of the di with an ever-expanding and shrinking continuum of plucked strings. From the performance of "Galloping on the Prairie", one cannot help but admire the dynamic leadership of He Wu-qi, who had such a wonderful handle on what made good music.

In 1978, the Chinese Music Society of North America produced an audio-visual program illustrating Chinese orchestration using the music "Fishing Song of the East China Sea" and synchronized 35mm slides which explained the orchestration. The program was very well received from coast to coast. It provided the audience with the background to properly appreciate the performing arts of the Chinese orchestra. The "Fishing Song of the East China Sea" created in its listener the broadest range of perception from the most lyrical melodic progression to highly symphonic tonal and dynamic contrast.

The use of tonal contrast can be appreciated by examining the beginning passage of the "Fishing Song of the East China Sea". Transparent voice of the sheng's without vibrato in displaced registers

(Shen, 1980) are echoed by the awakening sound of the large hai-luo. This is followed by alternately crisp and muffed sound of the yangqin:

The di then emerges with tremendous embodied power:

backed by the plucked strings.

Apart from the tremendous tonal and dynamic interest, the "Fishing Song of the East China Sea" offers the most beautiful melody:

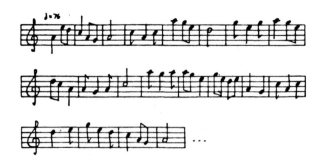

Shanghai Traditional Orchestra

Such simple but genuinely musical development is rare in today's repertoire. The "Fishing Song of the East China Sea" provides a good testing ground for inter-modal development. It continuously spans the domain of two harmonic groups, e.g. E-yu and B-jue (For definition of the harmonies, see Shen, 1981). The passage:

often provides a transition from jue to yu:

Another interesting observation is that the whole piece ends on a jue harmony, which is consistent with the inter-modal development between the jue and the yu harmonies often observed in classical compositions.

FUTURE IN PERSPECTIVE

Under He Wu-qi's leadership, the Shanghai Traditional Orchestra prospered in all directions:

Chinese Music and Orchestration

1. It built a community of extremely creative musicians. There is evidence that the atmosphere then at the Shanghai Traditional Orchestra promoted close collaborations between composers and composers, and between performers and performers.

2. It performed, preserved, recorded, and created a broad range of excellent repertoire. Their best known recorded works appear below.

Ma An Shan Overture (Ma An Shan Xuqu)
Composed by He Wu-qi
    He Wu-qi, conductor
(Recorded about 1960)

Galloping on the Prairie
Composed by Lu Chun-ling and Gu Guanren
    Lu Chun-ling, di
    He Wu-qi, conductor
(Recorded about 1960)

Fishing Song of the East China Sea
Composed by Ma Shenglong and Gu Guanren
    He Wu-qi, conductor
(Recorded about 1960)

Xiao He Tang Shui
Music of Yunnan
Arrangement by Pan Miao-xing and Zhang Shirui
    Pan Miao-xing, liuqin
(Recorded about 1960)

The Four Season Melody (Si Ji Diao)

Shanghai Traditional Orchestra

Music of Qinghai
Arrangement by Zeng Jia-qing
   He Wu-qi, conductor

Going to the Fair (Gan Ji)
Shuangtiaogu Music of Anhui
Arrangement by Zeng Jia-qing
   Jiang Xuan-feng, erhu
   Xiang Zuhua, yangqin

Song of Joy (Huan Le Ge)
Music of southern Jiangsu (Jiangnan)
(Recorded about 1960)

Zhonghua Liuban
Music of southern Jiangsu (Jiangnan)
(Recorded about 1960)

Dadu River (Dadu He)
Music by Luo Zhongxian, Shi Lemeng and Chan Tianhe
Arrangement by Zeng Jia-qing

The Great Ambuscade (Shi Mian Mai Fu)
   Tang Liangxing, pipa
(Recorded 1974)

Xian Hua Diao
Music of Northern Jiangsu
Arrangement by Zeng Jia-qing
   He Wu-qi, conductor

Chinese Music and Orchestration

My Brother Comes Home (Gege Hui Lai Liao)
Composed by Zhang Changchen
Accompaniment arranged by Gu Guanren
    Xiao Bai-yong, erhu
    Xiang Zuhua, yangqin

The Flower Does Not Bloom Before the Hero Arrives
Composed by Tang Chongxi
Arrangement by Gu Guanren
    Ma Shenglong, conductor

Purple Bamboo Melody (Zi Zhu Diao)
Music of Shanghai Opera (Huju)
Arrangement by Ma Shenglong
(Recorded 1977)

Zhonghua Liuban
Music of southern Jiangsu (Jiangnan)
    Lu Chun-ling, di
    Zhou Hui, yangqin
(Recorded 1960)

Wedding Processional (Xinjie)
Music of southern Jiangsu (Jiangnan)
(Recorded 1960)

Trip to Suzhou (Gusu Xin)
Music of Kun Opera (Kunqu)
Arrangement by Jiang Xianwei
    Yu Xunfa, di

Shanghai Traditional Orchestra

(Recorded 1975)

Mile After Mile of Green Mountain
Music of Inner Mongolia

Today maestro He Wu-qi is no longer with us. To encourage the new generation of Musicians, I would like to list below tasks, that the Shanghai Traditional Orchestra has not done or has not been able to complete, that will greatly benefit the world in terms of making available the fruits of the human civilization.

1. The propagation and institutionalization in a systematic manner the tradition of the silk and bamboo compositions. The Shanghai Traditional Orchestra has been the closest professional organization to the semiprofessional silk and bamboo community which flourished in the first two-thirds of the twentieth century.

2. The propagation and institutionalization of wind and percussion music of Jiangsu and Zhejiang. A good understanding of wind and percussion instrumentation of Jiangsu and Zhejiang was well demonstrated in compositions of the Shanghai Traditional Orchestra in the 1950s and 1960s. The "Fishing Song of the East China Sea" is an excellent example.

By institutionalization I mean the complete procedure of analysis, documentation, theory formation, performance, recording, textbook development, and instruction.

The news of He Wu-qi's death came too late for a proper obituary. Measuring our appreciation of the work of his generation of musicians, this paper is long overdue. If the items listed above as work that was rendered incomplete due to unfortunate societal chaos could be achieved in the next three to five years, the Shanghai Traditional Orchestra will no doubt set an example of an institution of integrity and responsibility in the history of civilization.

Is what I hoped above possible? The human resource, although scarcer than fifteen years ago, exists. It is up to the new generation of the Shanghai Traditional Orchestra to demonstrate their leadership, world outlook, and cooperative ingenuities.

REFERENCES

Shen, Sin-yan, Foundations of the Chinese Orchestra (2), *Chinese Music*, 3/1, 16 (1980).

Shen, Sin-yan, What Makes Chinese Music Chinese? *Chinese Music*, **4**/2, 23 (1981).

Appendix I: Instruments of the Orchestra

APPENDIX I: INSTRUMENTS OF THE ORCHESTRA[10]

Chinese music is one of the oldest and most highly developed musical traditions. The earliest documented music-making activities involved the use of wind instruments and percussion instruments including the xun (globular flute), paixiao (panpipe), sheng (mouth organ), qing (stone chime), gu (drum), zhong (bell chime), zhu and wu (both percussion idiophones) and others. The earliest xuns unearthed, dating back to 5,000 BC, have tone sequences based primarily on a minor-third system. Chinese musical compositions utilize a comprehensive system of harmonies, whose skeletons are listed below, built upon both fourths and thirds:

zhi harmony: sol-do-re-sol
shang harmony: re-sol-la-re
yu harmony: la-re-mi-la
jue harmony: mi-la-do-mi
gong harmony: do-mi-sol-do

The Chinese system of tuning encompasses the closest approximations to the just intervals. Depending on the melodic progression, scale pitches are selected from 23 different steps within the octave so that each principal interval in the progressing is just. The 23 steps within the

---

[10] Originally published in *Chinese Music*, Vol. 7, No. 2 (1984).

Chinese Music and Orchestration

octave are respectively (in cents): 90, 114, 180, 204, 294, 384, 408, 474, 498, 588, 612, 678, 702, 792, 816, 882, 906, 972, 996, 1086, 1110, 1176 and 1200. This system is known as the Pan Huai-su pure temperaments.

Orchestral, ensemble and solo instrumental music of China are considered one of the highest art forms of the world. Multipart formal design dominates this category of Chinese music. A four-stage development is often used in melodic design: qi (introduction), cheng (elucidation of the theme), zhuan (transition to another viewpoint) and he (summing up).

Chinese instruments are classified according to acoustical material: e.g.

metal:	zhong, nao (cymbal), bo (cymbal), yunluo (gong chime), daluo (large gong)
stone:	qing
clay:	xun
leather:	gu, sanxian (three-stringed long-necked lute) erhu (python-skin fiddle), jinghu (bamboo fiddle)
silk:	qin (seven-stringed zither without bridges), se (open-stringed zither with bridges), banhu (wood fiddle), erhu, zhuihu, yangqin (hammered dulcimer), liuqin (small lute), pipa (pear-shaped grand lute), ruan (round lute), sanxian
wood:	zhu, wu, gu, ban (clapper), muyu (slit-drum), qin, se banhu, erhu, zhuihu, yangqin, liuqin, pipa, ruan, sanxian
gourd:	sheng, yu (mouth organs)
bamboo:	xiao (vertical flute), di (transverse flute), paixiao

and according to playing techniques:

Appendix I: Instruments of the Orchestra

wind:	di, xiao, sheng, suona (shawm), guan (cylindrical oboe), bawu (flute with single free reed)
percussion:	gu, ban, bo, yunluo, daluo
plucked:	yangqin, liuqin, pipa, ruan, sanxian, zheng
bowed:	banhu, erhu, jinghu, zhuihu.

Chinese orchestration is based on the use of si (silk), zhu (bamboo), chui (reeded wind) and da (percussion) tonal components, and tonal interest presides over melodic or harmonic interest in orchestral interpretations. The masterly and meticulous use of tonal interest is evident throughout Chinese instrumental repertoire. The Chinese string quartet (xian-suo), for example, uses a fiddle (to provide bowed sound), a horizontal open-stringed wooden zither and two plucked lutes of different timbre (one fretted and wooden with a rounded back and the other finger-boarded with a python-skin resonator), The spectrum of musical effects resulting from the available timbre and playing techniques provides an endless source of musical interest.

banhu High-pitched Chinese bowed-string instrument used all over China, especially popular in Northern China. It has two strings stretched over a small bamboo bridge resting on a wooden soundboard which forms the front of a circular soundbox fabricated from a coconut shell. It is played vertically with the bow running between the strings and bowing is done close to the top of the resonator. The bridge is placed about a fifth the diameter of the resonator from the top of the resonator. It is the leading bowed string in the accompanying orchestra of several regional operas. A soprano version tuned a fifth apart (d-a, with bottom note an octave and a whole step above middle C) and an alto version tuned a fourth apart (b flat-e flat) are popular. Its performance is characterized by frequent use of rapid separate-bowing and glissandos.

Chinese Music and Orchestration

Best known performers in the 20th century include Liu Ming-yuan, Zhang Chang-cheng, Yan Shao-i, Gu Da-ru and others.

bawu Chinese single free-reed wind instrument. An instrument popular in Southwestern China played in a manner similar to playing the flute except all air passes through a single pointed reed at the mouth-hole. The tone produced is a result of the coupling between the reed and the air column. The common F bawu has a lowest pitch of middle C and spans a compass of more than two octaves. Its performance is characterized by colorful tonal contrast, glissandos, various tonguing and fingering techniques, and circular breathing. Well-known artists include Yan Tie-ming, Zhang Zu-yu and others.

di Also known as dizi, a generic name for the Chinese side-blown flutes. The instrument has a reed-membrane covering a hole so the tone produced is a result of the coupling between the air column and the reed-membrane. There are usually six finger-holes on the cylindrical body made of bamboo or wood. There are many sizes of Chinese flutes. The common soprano flute has a lowest pitch of d (an octave plus a whole step above middle C) and the common alto flute has a lowest pitch of a (first octave above middle C). The playing range is about two octaves plus a fifth. Special techniques of performance include circular breathing for extensive passages, fluttered tonguing, double tonguing, triple tonguing, and many combinations of fingering and tonguing techniques. Best known performers in the 20th century include Lu Chun-ling, Feng Zi-chun, Wang Tie-chui and others.

erhu Chinese vertical fiddle without a fingerboard. It is the most popular Chinese fiddle which plays the role of the second bowed string in orchestration. It has two strings, tuned commonly to c-g or d-a (bottom note near middle C), stretched over a bridge which rests against

Appendix I: Instruments of the Orchestra

the python-skin membrane of a wooden drum-resonator. A vertical post with no fingerboard goes through the sides of the resonator and the bow runs between the strings. Bowing is done horizontally with right-hand fingering techniques for altering the bow tension and for crossing strings while the instrument is held vertically on the thigh. In addition to its orchestral role it is also a solo instrument with a large repertory. Its performance is characterized by subtle contrasts in bowing strength, powerful tension-altering vibrato, and a wide variety of glissandos. A higher-pitched version with a smaller resonator surface (and sometimes a bell-shaped body to give a broad dynamic range and short effective resonator length) is tuned g-d or a-e (a fourth to a fifth higher than the erhu) and is called the gaohu. In southern orchestras in China, the gaohu is often the first bowed string with the erhu being the second. Another lower-pitched version with a larger resonator than the erhu is the zhonghu and is tuned an octave lower than the gaohu. Several bass range versions are popular, including the dahu, dihu, gehu, and dige. Composers including A Bing, Liu Tian-hua, Liu Wen-jin, Zeng Jia-qing and others gave the erhu increased importance as a solo instrument.

guan Doubled-reed Chinese woodwind instrument with a cylindrical body and a large reed. It is the leading instrument of several regional Chinese orchestras. It has eight, nine or more finger holes and typically covers a range of two and a half octaves. Three sizes are common whose lowest pitches are a (below middle C), e, and a' (in first octave above middle C). A version in Southern China has a horn and smaller cylindrical body and is called the houguan. Well-known artists in the 20th century include Yin Er-wen, Zhang Ji-gui and others.

konghou Chinese multi-stringed plucked instrument of the harp family. It first appeared in the Han Period (206 BC - 220 AD) and was popular as an orchestral and a solo instrument until about the 14th century when

Chinese Music and Orchestration

its importance was superseded by other instruments. It became popular again in the twentieth century through its use by the Shanghai Traditional Orchestra and the Central Traditional Orchestra. Its sound box resembles that of a pipa but with a phoenix headed neck. On each side of the sound box is a row of bridges over which 36 strings are stretched. Fixed to the bridges is a device coordinating the two groups of strings in movements of pressing, kneading, trilling and sliding. Its range usually includes five and half octaves centered approximately at middle C. Its music is characterized by tension-altering embellishments, glissandos, arpeggiated chords and register contrast.

liuqin Also called liu-ye-qin, soprano lute of China. It is the highest-pitched member of the plucked string group of the Chinese orchestras. Four strings are stretched over a short bridge which rests near the bottom of the pear-shaped wooden soundboard which has two circular sound-holes. It is played with a small plectrum. The strings are tuned g-d-g'-d' (bottom note below middle C) or a-d-a'-d'. Its performance is characterized by rapid long-tremolos, crisp high-pitched tonal colors, and full-bodied chords. Its range covers three and a half octaves. Wang Hui-ran, Pan Miao-xing and others gave the liuqin increased importance as a solo instrument.

pipa Generic name for a large class of Chinese plucked lutes. The common version has a short neck, a pear-shaped body with a wooden belly. There are six convex frets on the neck and 23 frets on the belly. The four strings run from a fastener on the belly to conical tuning pegs in the sides of the bent-back pegbox. They are plucked with all five fingers of the right-hand while the instrument is held vertically on the thigh. It is present in most regional orchestras and is an important solo instrument with a large repertory. Its performance is characterized by repeated strumming utilizing fingers in a continuous roll, producing an

Appendix I: Instruments of the Orchestra

undulating long-tremolo, and chords made up of fourths, fifths and thirds. A common tuning is a-d-e-a' (top note below middle C). Another version has a round belly and a long neck and is known as the ruan, with four common sizes.

qin Chinese plucked string instrument with elongated trapezoidal and slightly arched wooden box resonator and seven strings but no bridges. The strings are plucked by the right-hand fingers while the left hand fingers stops the strings at desired lengths. Thirteen small ivory or mother-of-pearl disks inlaid in the resonator surface provide reference for the stopping points and positions of harmonics. Over two-hundred notations are used to indicate the playing technique, stopping position, and tonal requirements. The use of harmonics in melodic progression is a characteristic feature of compositions. A total of ninety-one choices is available. The open strings, the stopped pitches and the harmonics are used in contrast with each other. A very large repertory exists for this instrument and best known players include Si Kuang, Si Wen, Si Xiang (Spring and Autumn and the Warring States Period, 770 BC - 221 BC), Cai Wen-ji (177 AD -?, Han Period), Ji Kang (227 - 263 AD, Jin Period), Guo Chu-wang (1190 - 1260, Song Period, Wang Yan-qing (1866 - 1921), Guan Ping-hu (1887 - 1967), Zha Fu-xi (1895 - 1976), Wu Jing-lue (1906 -) and others.

sanxian Any of a group of long-necked, fretless Chinese lutes with three strings, a rectangular resonator with python skin front and back, and a curved-back pegbox with side pegs. The instrument is popular in theatrical accompaniment, ballad-singing accompaniment, and in the orchestra. The large san-xian is about 1.2 meters long and the small san-xian is about 0.96 meters long. Common tuning of the large san-xian is between D, A, d and G, d, g, and that of the small is between A, d, a, and d, a, d' (top note just above middle C). It has a compass

Chinese Music and Orchestration

of three octaves and is played with fingernails of the right hand. Its performance is characterized by powerful resonant rolls and chords and large glissandos on the finger-board. Bai Feng-yan (1899 - 1975), Li Yi (1932 -), and others gave the san-xian increased importance as a solo instrument.

sheng Chinese free-reeded mouth-organ. It is the first musical instrument in the world utilizing a coupled acoustical system, between an air column and free reed. A large number (17, 21, 36 are common) of bamboo pipes (each coupled to a corresponding free reed made of brass at its base) are mounted on its metallic wind-chest; an individual pipe sounds when its finger-hole is covered. It is a member of most regional orchestras of China and plays the crucial role of harmonizing the tonal color of different groups of instruments. Its performance is characterized by the frequent use of three-note harmony, fluttered-tonguing, long-tremolo, and short glissandos. Hu Tian-quan, Wang Qing-shen, Yan Hai-deng and others gave it increased importance as a solo instrument.

suona Double-reed Chinese woodwind instrument with a conical body (with a conical bore) made of wood, and a metallic horn and a small reed. It has eight basic finger-holes and typically covers a range of two octaves plus a whole step. It is the principal member of the reed-and-percussion type Chinese orchestra. Four sizes of the suona are common whose lowest pitches are respectively b (an octave and a semitone below middle C), e (a minor sixth below middle C), a (a minor third below middle C) and g (a fifth above middle C). It is characterized by its shrill sound and the frequent use of fluttered-tonguing in performance and its music frequently requires the use of circular-breathing. Zhao Chun-ting, Hao Yu-qi, Ren Tong-xiang, Hu Hai-quan and other gave it increased importance as a solo instrument.

Appendix I: Instruments of the Orchestra

yangqin Multi-stringed Chinese dulcimer in which tone is produced by struck strings. It is played with a pair of elastic bamboo strikers covered with rubber or leather. The vibration of the strings is transmitted to a trapezoidal wooden soundboard by means of bridges over which the strings are stretched. It is an important member of the Chinese orchestras and is popular in ballad singing accompaniments. The modern yangqin has four or five bridges with sets of strings on each bridge pitched whole steps apart and neighboring sets of strings on adjacent bridges pitched a fifth apart, thus allowing a complete chromatic scale to be played in all keys. Its range covers one octave below middle C and two and half octaves above. Yan Lao-lie, Chen De-ju, Xiang Zu-hua, Yang Jing-ming and others gave the yangqin increased importance as a solo instrument.

yunluo Chinese fixed-pitched gong chime consisting of a large number of gongs (36, 37 are common) of different thickness but similar surface area suspended on a wooden frame. It is played with a pair of small mallets (hard and soft ones are used). In orchestral performance, the yun-luo is used to play melodic passages as well as to outline harmonic skeletons. It has a large dynamic range and a large compass (usually three octaves) and is used as a solo instrument with the Chinese orchestras. A version with ten or more gongs of different surface areas is the shimianluo and is used for tonal decoration in orchestration.

zheng Chinese plucked string instrument with horizontal wooden box resonator and 16 to 21 or more strings stretched over individual bridges. The resonator has a slightly arched surface and is elongated-trapezoidal. The bottom is flat with sound holes. The playing range spans three to four octaves. Fingers of both hands may pluck to the right of the bridge, or the right fingers may pluck and the left fingers alter the string tension on the left side of the bridge under the plucked string to change

Chinese Music and Orchestration

the pitch or to provide embellishments. Its music is characterized by register contrast, two- to eight-note chords, arpeggiated chords, long-tremolos, and glissando. It is an important solo instrument, an accompaniment instrument for ballad singing, and an integral member of chamber ensembles and orchestras. Well-known performers include Cao Dong-fu (1898 - 1970), Zhao Yu-zhai (1923 -) and others.

Note: The most popular percussion instruments are discussed in chapter on "Orchestration with Chinese Percussion Instruments" in the form of glossaries, and are not repeated here.

Chinese Music and Orchestration

INDEX

- A -

A Bing, 122, 149
acoustics, 2, 8-10, 20, 32-34, 45-76, 100-127
    cultural, 2, 8-10, 20, 69, 73-75, 122-125
    artistic conception, 11-13

- B -

Bai Feng-yan, 152
banhu, 18, 24-25, 28, 30, 32, 121-122, 125-127, 147-148
    acoustics of, 121
    open-string tones, 121
    performance of - in *The Little Cowherd*, 18
    special performing technique of, 121
Bangzi, clapper opera, 23, 25, 27, 32, 119
    Henan, (or Yuju), 23, 25, 27
    Shaanxi, (or Qinqiang), see Shaanxi Bangzi
bawu, free-reed flute, 49, 56, 68-69, 125, 148
    performance of, 68-69
    with erhu, 125
Benade, Arthur, 125
bili, 73
Birds Return to the Woods, 123
bo, a large class of Chinese cymbals, see cymbals

Book of Songs, 103
Book of History, 103
Boston Symphony, 12
bowed strings (huqin), 24-25, 31-32, 48, 54, 59, 117-138
    artistry of Chinese fiddles, 120-125
    banhu, see banhu
    ensemble roles, 125-127
    erhu, see erhu
    erxian, see erxian
    gaohu (yuehu), see gaohu
    general design, 117
    in different types of orchestras, 24-25
    jinghu, 119, 126
    performing techniques, 118
    piaohu, 30
    touxian, 119
    zhonghu, 24-25, 32, 54, 127
    zhuihu, see zhuihu

- C -

cadence, 5
Cai Wen-ji, 151
Cantonese music (Guangdong music), 22, 24, 26, 35-36, 119
Cao Dong-fu, 154
Ce sha, see side cadence
Changxi opera, see Xi opera

Chao-zhou (Teo-chew), 22-27, 119
    music of, 22, 24, 26, 119
    Reed & Percussion School of, 23, 25, 27
Chaoju (Chao opera), 32
chaoluo, 92
    different sized, 92
    use in symphony, 92
Chen De-ju, 153
chi, closed-tubed transverse flute, 66
chiba, Southern styled end-blown flute (shakuhachi in Japan), 62
Chinese orchestra, 14-43, 45-60, 75-76, 89-99, 100-114, 125-130, 145-154
    acoustical space, 45-60
    bowed strings in, 54-55, 75-76, 125-130
    comparison with Western symphony, 13, 31, 47-48, 52, 55, 57, 80, 87, 92, 114, 125
    foundations of, 14-43
    instruments of, 145-154
    percussions in, 30-31, 89-99
    plucked strings in, 31-37, 100-114
    types of, 21-31
    wind instruments in, 37-43, 72-76
Chuida (reed & percussion), 21-29, 41-43
    instrumentation of 29
    orchestra of 21-29
    of Chao-zhou, 23, 25, 27
    of Northern China, 22, 24, 26
    of southern Jiangsu Province (Sunan Chuida), 22, 24, 26, 29
    of Zhejiang Province, 22, 24, 26
clarinet, 65
cultural acoustics, see acoustics

cymbal (bo), 85 (picture), 89-90, 92

- D -

Dance of Yao, The, 39, 41, 43
Dagger Society, The, 41-42
daluo, large gong, 83, 90-92
    performance of, 83
daruan, large ruan, 56, 58
di, transverse flute with reed membrane, 22-23, 29, 31, 49-50, 56, 65-66, 69, 135-138, 146, 148
    acoustical design, 67
    in orchestration, 31, 49-50, 56, 135, 137, 138
    sound of, 68
    with the pressured reed, 50
    duets, 50
dizi, see di
dominant, 3, 6-7
    fifth, 3, 6
    minor sixth, 7
dongxiao, see xiao
double reed, 41-43, 71-72
    flattened, 71
    music of, 71-72
    unflattened, 71
drum (gu), 31, 86, 87-89
    danpigu, 31, 87, 88 (picture)
    ganggu, 86 (picture), 91

guban, 87, 88 (picture)
paigu, 31
tanggu, 31, 86-87, 89 (picture), 91
Dui Hua (Flower Riddles), 16-17
    analysis of harmony structure, 16-17

- E -

edge effect, 62-64, 66
Eight Suites of Shanxi Province, 22, 24, 26
    The, 22, 24, 26
equal temperament, 58, 60, 123
    in musical space, 58, 60
    in performance, 123
erhu, 18, 28, 30, 32, 45-60, 75-76, 118-121, 141-142, 146-147, 148-149
    as color instrument, 54
    changcheng erhu, 120
    ensemble roles of, 125-127
    Fantasy on the Sanmen Gorge, 123
    fixed position glissando, 122-123
    in ensemble, 28, 30, 32, 45-60, 75-76, 114, 125, 126-127
    Moon Mirrored in Erquan, The 122, 124
    performance of - in *The Little Cowherd*, 18
    temperament, 123
    resonator, 126
    special performing technique, 124
    spectrum, 54-55
    tuoyin erhu, 119
    zhuyin erhu, 119
Erjiaxian, 129
erxian, 119

- F -

Feng Zi-chun, 148
fiddle, see bowed strings
Fishing Song of the East China Sea, 37-38, 52, 55, 94, 137-139, 140, 143
fifth, 6, 15, 19, 59, 87, 94, 129, 147, 149, 151, 152, 153
Flower Riddles, see *Dui Hua*
Flower Drum opera, 23, 25, 27
    of Hunan, 23, 25, 27
flute, see also di and wind, 62-67
    acoustical design, 65-67
    bone, 8000 years old, 63
    globular, see xun
    scientific breakthrough, 65-67
    side-blown, 66
    transverse, 65
    vertical, 62, 63-64
fourth, 6, 7, 10, 15, 19, 50, 59, 119, 121, 129, 145, 147, 149, 151
    in performing technique of fiddles, 121
Fujian province, 22-27, 30-31
    Southern music (Nan music) of, 22, 24, 26
    Liyuan opera of, 23, 25, 27, 30-31

- G -

Chinese Music and Orchestration

gaohu, high-registered Cantonese fiddle, 59, 119, 125-127
    ensemble roles of, 126-127
glissando, 122
    fixed position glissando (dingba huayin), 122
    padded glissando (dianzhi huayin), 122
gong, 83, 84, 92-93
gong chime, 82, 84-85, 97, 153
    shimianluo, different tone colored gong chime, 82 (picture), 97
    yunluo, fixed pitched gong chime, 84 (picture), 84-85, 97, 153
grace note, 18, 124
Great Wall, The, 120, 122
gu, a large class of Chinese drums, see drum
Gu Da-ru, 148
Gu Guanren, 37-38, 133-134, 140, 142
guan (guanzi), unflattened double reed with cylindrical resonator, 22, 23, 29, 37, 41-42, 49, 69-73, 147, 149
    in orchestras, 22-23
    reed of, 71
Guan Ping-hu, 151
guanyue, Chinese wind group, 72, 75
Guangdong music (Cantonese music), 22, 24, 26, 35-36, 119
guitar-like resonator, 112
Guo Chu-wang, 151

- H -

haidi, 22-23, 37, 41-42, 49
Han Dynasty, 107-108, 115 149, 151
Hao Yu-qi, 152
harmony, 2-10, 16-20, 31, 37, 50, 58, 59, 65, 69, 139, 145, 152
    basis set, 3-10, 17
    Chinese preference of, 2-10
    comprehensive set of, 2
    cyclic system, 9
    gong, 6, 7, 8
    in Western classical music system, 9-10, 20
    jue, 6, 7, 139
    relation to different cultures, 15
    shang, 5, 8
    system, definition, 14
    yu, 6, 8, 20
    zhi, 3, 4, 8, 19, 20
Henan Ballad Singing, 22, 24, 26, 114, 119, 129
    Henan Zhuizi, 119, 129
    Pre-curtain music of (Bantouqu), 22, 24, 26, 114
Henan Bangzi opera, 23, 25, 27, 29, 30
Henan Province, 86
    Yin Ruins of Anyang, 86
He Wu-qi, 37, 132-144
Hou Jiuxia, 28
houguan, 22-23, 41-42, 49
Hu Hai-quan, 152
Hu Tian-quan, 152
Huaguxi, see Flower Drum opera

Huju, see Shanghai opera
hulei, see hulei, under plucked strings
Hunan Province, 23, 25, 27
    Flower Drum opera of, 23, 25, 27
Huqin (the Chinese vertical fiddle group), see bowed strings

- I -

institutionalization, 122
intervals, 2-10, 15, 46, 57-58, 62-66, 69, 122, 123, 128, 145-146
    cultural preference, 2, 15, 46, 57, 62-65, 69
    equal-tempered, 58
    in Chi performance, 66
    in Chinese tuning, 145-146
    in fixed position glissando, 122
    in sheng performance, 69
    in wind performance, 62, 63
    in zhuihu performance, 128
    just intervals and subdivision, 63, 123
interval music, 56-58

- J -

Jazz,
    musicians and suona, 74
Ji Kang, 151
Jiangnan (southern Jiangsu Province), 35-37, 40, see also silk & bamboo

Joy of Xiangjiang, 124

- K -

Kenzo, Hayashi, 72
konghou, 59, 149 (glossary)
kouxian, see vibrato, tension-altering
Kunqu, 29, 31, 142
    influence on Sizhu orchestras, 29

- L -

Li Bing-yuan, 124
Li Yi, 152
ling, 85 (picture), 86, 95
Little Cowherd, (Xiao Fangniu), 18-19
    performance of erhu and banhu in the, 18
Liu Ming-yuan, 117, 121, 148
Liu Tian-hua, 119, 149
Liu Tian-Yi, 117, 121, 123
Liu Tieshan, 39
Liu Wen-jin, 30, 52, 58, 99, 120, 149
liuqin, 26, 27, 32, 47, 51-53, 56, 101, 110, 113, 150
Liuqin opera, 23, 25, 27
Liuyang River, 20
    analysis of harmony structure, 20
Liyuan Opera (Liyuanxi), 23, 25, 27, 30-31
    of Fujian Province, 23, 25, 27, 30-31
Liyuanxi, see Liyuan Opera
Luju (Shandong Province), 119

Lu Chun-ling, 66, 133, 148

- M -

*Ma An Shan Overture,
The*, 134-137
Ma Shenglong, 37-39, 52, 55, 133, 134, 140
Mao Yuan, 39, 142
major second, 63
major third, 9, 10
major triad, 8
Meihua Sannong, 57
melodic progression, 4, 14, 16-18, 69, 136-137, 145
miao (sound pipe of sheng), 40
minor sixth, 7
minor third, 2-3, 6-7, 9-10, 63-64, 66, 121-122, 124
    in fiddle performance, 121-122, 124
    in jue and gong harmony, 6, 7
    on seven thousand years old globular flute, 2, 64
    preference of, 2-3, 6, 9, 66
minor triad, 7, 20
Moon on High, 95
*Moon Mirrored in Erquan,
The*, 122, 124
Music at Sunset, 11-12
musical language, 56-58
    intervals in, 57-58
musical psychology, 48, 52, 54-59
musical space, 56-58

Chinese, 56-58

- N -

Needham, Joseph, 66

- O -

oboe, 65, 75
octave, 57
    in Chinese musical language, 57
    unequal, 57
open-string resonance, see resonance
orchestra, 21-31
    Chuida (reed and percussion), 21-29
    Sizhu (silk and bamboo), 21, 28
    types of, 21-31
ornamentation, 18
    in *The Little Cowherd*, 18
    of the performer, 18
overtone, 75-76
Ozawa, Seiji, 12

- P -

paigu, fixed pitched drum set, 55
paixiao, panpipe, 62, 64, 67
Pan Miao-xing, 133, 140, 150
*Pearl Tower,
the*, 28, 29

Peking opera (Jingju), 15, 23, 25, 27, 30, 31, 87, 93, 119
Peng Xiuwen, 39, 95
percussions, 21, 26-27, 29-31, 46, 55-56, 80-99, 126-127, 135, 137, 143, 146-147
    basic effects, 81
    flexibility and creativity of percussion music, 55
    in different types of orchestras, 26-27, 30
    orchestration with, 80-99
    pitch, 29
    pitch space, 56
    range in Chuida, 29
percussion patterns, 16
piccolo, 65
pipa, 11, 21, 26-30, 51, 52, 56, 58, 59, 76, 100-116, 118, 126, 129, 141, 146, 147, 150
    dipolar sound radiation, 52
    in different types of orchestras, 26, 27
    in Kunqu, 29
    use of - in tanci, 28-29
Pingju, 23, 30
plucked strings, 32-36, 100-116
    classification of, 105
    development of, 106
    fingerboard, 101, 105
    fretted, 101, 105, 107
    hulei, 112
    huobusi, 112
    open string, 100, 105
    pipa, see pipa
    qin, see qin
    resonator of, 106, 108-109, 112
    ruan, see ruan
    strings used on, 107
    yangqin, see yangqin
    yueqin, see yueqin
    zheng, see zheng
    zhongruan, see zhongruan

- Q -

qin, 12, 52, 103, 105, 151
Qing Dynasty, 62
Qinqiang, see Shaanxi Bangzi
quality of music, 10-13
    Chinese, 10-13

- R -

recorder, 67
Ren Tong-xiang, 152
resonator, 32, 41-42, 48, 50, 58-59, 61-67, 112-113, 126, 129
    guitar-like, 112
    of erhu, 126
    of plucked strings, 50-51, 113
    of wind instruments, 41-42, 61-67
    of zhuihu, 129
resonance, 32, 49, 121, 127
    open-string, 121, 127
    of free-reed and air-column, 49

Rain Falls on the Plantains, 36
reed & percussion orchestra (Chuida orchestra), 21-29
    instrumentation of 29
    of Chao-zhou (teo-chew), 23, 25, 27
    of Northern China, 22, 24, 26
    of southern Jiangsu Province (Sunan Chuida), 22, 24, 26, 29
    of Zhejiang Province, 22, 24, 26
ruan, 26-27, 32, 108-111, 113
    marriage of ruan and pipa, 109-111

- S -

sanxian, 11, 22-29, 32-35, 52-53, 57, 60, 102, 104, 104, 108, 113-115, 130, 135, 148-149, 151
    in Kunqu, 29
    in Tanci, 28-29, 32-34
    large, 34
    small, 28
saxophone, 65
scale, 3-10, 57, 122
    heptatonic, 3-8
    pentatonic, 3, 9
Shaanxi Bangzi (Qinqiang), 2, 23, 25, 27, 32, 119
Shang Dynasty, 86
Shang Yi, 41
Shanghai opera (Huju), 23, 25, 27
Shanghai Opera's Traditional Orchestra, 41
Shanghai Traditional Orchestra, 11, 33, 37, 39

sheng, free-reeded mouthorgan, 22-23, 29, 30-31, 37-41, 45-60, 64-69, 74, 114, 134, 136, 135, 146-148, 152 (glossary)
    gaoyinsheng, lusheng, susheng, zhongyinsheng, 39-40, 49
    harmonies performed on, 38
    performance, 64
    sound of, 68
    structure of, 40, 64, 152
sheng-guan (shengguan), Chinese reeded wind family, 45-60, 72-75, 125
    as fundamental spectrum group in orchestra, 47-48, 48-50
Si Kuang, 151
Si Wen, 151
Si Xiang, 151
side cadence, 5, 6
side-blown excitation, 66
silk and bamboo (Sizhu), 21, 22, 35, 66, 80, 125, 132, 135-137
    of Jiangnan, 21, 22, 24, 26, 28, 35-37
Sizhu, see silk and bamboo
Song Dynasty, 31, 65, 153
Southern music (Nan music), 22, 24, 26
    of Fujian Province, 22, 24, 26
Spring to a Hundred Households, 95
Spring at the Emerald Lake, 5
subdominant, 3, 6-7
    fourth, 6-7
Sunan Chuida, see Chuida of southern Jiangsu
suona, 22-23, 29-31, 38, 41-42, 50, 57, 60, 66, 72, 74-76, 149, 152
    in different types of orchestras, 22, 23, 29

system, 114

- T -

tan, downward pluck movement, 101-102
Tanci, 28-29
    use of sanxian and pipa, 28-29
Tang Dynasty, 108, 112, 115
Tang Kaixuan, 97
tanbo, Chinese plucked string family, 47-48, 50-59
    as fundamental spectrum group in orchestra, 47-48, 50-59
    tonal spectrum of, 47-48, 52
    with violin group, 52
tanggu, see drum
tantiao, plucking technique, see also tan and tiao, 102
tantiao system, 28, 51, 52, 100-116, see also tanbo
    in Tanci, 28
    dipolar type, 52
tao (taogu, or xiantao), 33, 103-104
    ancient sanxian, 103
taogu, see tao
Teo-chew, see Chao-zhou
temperament, 123
    equal temperament, see equal temperament
    in fiddle performance, 123
tertian structure, 3, 7
third, 9-10
    major, 9, 10
    minor, see minor third
tiao, upward pluck movement, 101-102
tonal contrast, 50
tonal interest, 10-13, 21, 28, 31, 34, 37, 47-60, 62-63, 76, 75, 81-87, 93, 106, 112, 121-127
    fiddles, 121-127
    frets vs. fingerboard, 106
    percussions, 81-87, 93
    tonal manipulation, 10
tonal spectrum, 46-50
    fundamental spectrum, 47-48
    of an orchestra, 47-48
    of shengguan, 48-50
    of tanbo, 50-52
    of Western symphony, 47
    supplementary spectrum, 47-48, 54-56
tonality (diaoxing), 3, 4, 6, 8, 16-20, 69, 145
    harmonic basic set and, 3, 4, 6, 8, 16-20, 69, 145
tone quality, 32-33, 41-43, 47-49, 67-69, 71-75
    double reed, 41-43, 71-72, 74-75
    free reed, 48-49, 67-69, 74
    globular flute (xun), 73
    membraned fiddle, 75-76
    membraned plucked string, 32-33
    unflattened double reed, 71, 73
    wood boxed resonator, 47
touxian, first fiddle of Chao-zhou music, 32, 119
tuning, 28, 119-120, 124, 129, 145-146, 150-152
    Chinese system, 145-146

erhu, 119-120, 124
pipa, 150-151
sanxian, 151-152
string instruments 59
yangqin, 28
zheng, 28
zhongruan, 59
zhuihu, 129

- U -

U-tube, 65-66
  in the mouthorgan, 65-66
Unforgettable Water Splashing Festival, 52, 99
  The, 52, 99

- V -

vibrato, 117, 127
  rolling, 127
  tension-altering (kouxian), 117, 127
violin, 45, 47-48, 52-54, 72, 118, 121-122, 124
  Chinese violin school, 124
  with tanbo group, 52

- W -

Wang Dian-yu, 129
Wang Guo-tong, 117, 121
Wang Hui-ran, 150

Wang Qing-shen, 152
Wang Tie-chui, 66, 148
Wang Yan-qing, 151
Wedding Processional, 34-35, 133, 142
wind instruments, 22-23, 61-79
  di, see di
  suona, see suona
  suona (high), 22-23
  suona (low), 22-23
  haidi, see haidi
  guan, see guan
  houguan, see houguan
  xiaodi, 22-23
  sheng, see sheng
  lusheng, see sheng
  xianfeng, munzi, haotong, zhaojun, dahao, hailuo, 22-23
  xiao, see xiao
  xun, see xun
Wu Jing-lue, 151

- X -

Xi opera (Changxi opera), 23, 25, 27
Xiang Zu-hua, 133, 153
xiantao, see tao
xiao, or dongxiao, Northern styled end-blown flute, 22-23, 29, 62
xiaoluo, small gong, 56, 84, 92-94
  in orchestra, 93-94
  performance of, 84
  sound of, 92-94

Xinying Traditional Orchestra, 34
xun, globular flute, 2, 62-63, 64, 73

- Y -

Yan Hai-deng, 152
Yan Lao-lie, 153
Yan Shao-i, 148
Yan Tie-ming, 148
Yang Jing-ming, 153
yangqin, 21, 26-28, 35-37, 51, 56, 59, 76, 95, 100, 102-103, 126, 138, 141, 142, 146-147, 153
    in different types of orchestras, 26, 27, 28
    in Jiangnan silk and bamboo, 21, 35-27
yi, see artistic conception
yin (sound or message), 10
Yin Er-wen, 149
Yin Ruins, 86
yu, free reeded mouth organ for melodic performance, 56, 65-66
    U-tube of, 66
yue (music), 10
Yue opera (Yueju), 22, 24, 26, 30, 32
    Lyrical orchestra of, 22, 24, 26
Yueju, see Yue opera
yueqin, 28, 32, 101, 102, 108, 113
yunluo, see gong chime
Yuju, see Henan Bangzi opera

Zeng Jia-qing, 133, 149
Zenghou Yi, 62-64, 66
    chi of, 66
    paixiao of, 62
Zha Fu-xi, 151
Zhang Chang-cheng, 148
Zhang Zu-yu, 148
Zhang Ji-gui, 149
Zhao Chun-ting, 152
Zhao Yu-zhai, 154
zheng sha (cadence), 5
zheng, 12, 20-21, 26-28, 30, 32, 51-52, 56, 59, 65, 100, 102, 103, 114, 147, 153
    in different types of orchestras, 26-27
    in Jiangnan silk and bamboo, 28
Zhonghua Liuban (Moderately Embellished Six Measures), 34, 133, 141, 142
zhongruan, 21, 51, 52, 56, 58-59
    energetic instrument, 59
Zhou Jiangzhou, 4
zhuihu (zhuizi), first fiddle of the Luju Opera, 32, 119, 128-129
    resonator of, 129

- Z -

ABOUT THE AUTHOR

Born in 1949 to Shanghainese parents, Sin-yan Shen studied music at very early age, mastering the vertical fiddle family of instruments. His dual career in music and physics culminated in the development of cultural acoustics, a discipline addressing scientifically the cultural molding of our ears and brain when it comes to music. Dr. Shen's life-long work centers on the question of "what music really is?" His teaching in North America and abroad has created a new understanding of music, its creative and social functions, and provides inspiration to a new generation of composers and music practitioners.

Dr. Sin-yan Shen pioneered the teaching of cultural acoustics at Northwestern and Harvard. He is currently Music Director of the Silk and Bamboo Ensemble and the Chinese Classical Orchestra, both touring internationally under the auspices of the Chinese Music Society of North America. He is editor of the international journal *Chinese Music*, music authority for the Encyclopedia Britannica, and a Fulbright Scholar. He serves as Technical Advisor to the Shanghai Musical Instruments Factory.